Writing/Home

Is a collection of writing by people from Teesside, on the subject of their homes and the associated pleasures, worries and conflicts. For some people home is a refuge, for some it is a prison, and for some it is both at the same time.

Contributors to this book include disabled people, people who have experienced mental health problems, people coming to this country through marriage, refugees and asylum seekers, a man who lived in a tree, a man of 102, a woman who grew up in a palace in Venice – many different people with many different viewpoints.

Some of the pieces are sad, some bitter, some regretful, some hopeful, some happy. all are deeply felt and personal.

Some contributors wrote in groups supported by locally established writers – Norah Hill, Andy Croft, Dougy Pincott and Val Magee. Some wrote as individuals, or dictated their pieces to me directly; most had never 'written' anything before, in the formal sense. I'm very grateful to everyone involved for their work, their openness, their willingness to share their experiences and thoughts. Thanks also to all supporting organisations.

Many thanks to Kirsten Lambird for her illustrations and cover design.

Rowena Sommerville
Cleveland Arts, May 2002

aunty's clean
house.
            .
            .
            .
every thing   .
in it's place. ....:

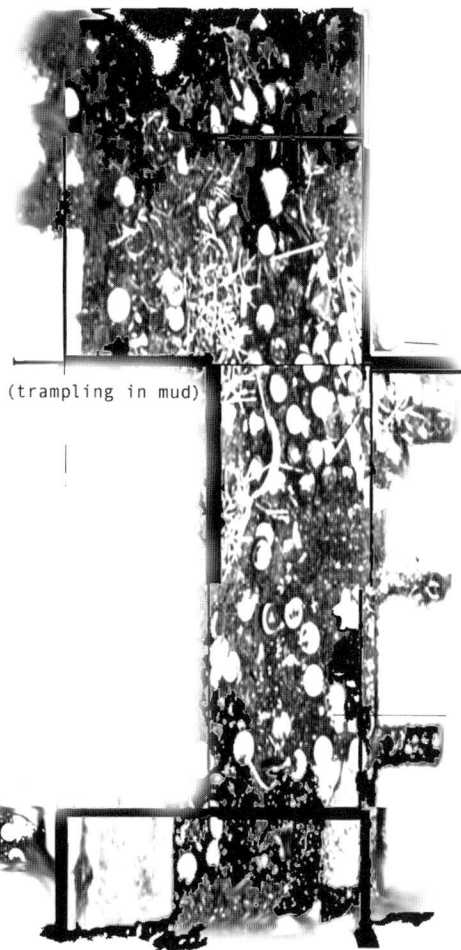

(trampling in mud)

Home

Home is not a building
Or a place to me
Home is in my head.
No-one can penetrate
Unless I allow them
Home is me
Anyone can enter into my house
Only those I choose come home.

Susan

How can I feel at home when I don't know if my children have a home;
how can I eat when I don't know if my children eat?

Ralph Olombi

My Home

My home
My castle
My fortress
My jail

My children
My life
My desperation
My solitude

My hopes
My nightmares
My dreams
My loneliness

Una

Home baked Bread

I am five years old.
I am sitting in the front room, watching the telly.
My mother is in the kitchen, cooking bread.
The smell of the bread drifts through the house,
Me and my sister are buzzing
As the bread will soon be cooked and ready to eat.
The smells of yeast, dough rising.
My mother keeps coming in to make sure that we are OK.
The smells of baking drift into all the rooms,
Our taste buds are pulsing
With the thought of home-made bread.

Darren

Home

If you are at peace with yourself
Content within your own way,
That makes you feel at home,
No matter what, or where you stay.

Ibsy

Homelessness

For a year, I've struggled against being homeless, to get out of that situation and it's been very hard. I finally moved out of bed and breakfast places, and hostels, which was really hard to do, but I went to my new home - I was really over the moon with it. At last, after all that time, I did achieve what I really wanted. I couldn't wait to move in and have a place to myself, I suppose mainly because it would be private and secure. Somewhere where I could take my children, which would be safe and happy instead of walking round the shops. It was worse when it was cold - it would be my chance to get them back and build a new life together.

But after being in my new home a year and a half, being there and working with social workers and officials, I'm doing really well and don't need so much help. This may mean I cannot stay in my new home. It's come full circle, really.

Another way of putting it is: as I now need less help from officials, there's some doubt that I will be allowed to stay in my supported accommodation. This means that my long efforts to escape homelessness have ironically made me homeless again.

People who make no effort to come out of homelessness, are really better off in the end, because they are officially deemed to be helpless; therefore they need more help. But if you're prepared to help yourself, they take the view that that person is no longer helpless, and so you are not getting help.

I will know my future in April when my case will be re-assessed.

....

When I found out that I could stay in my home, I felt so relieved and happy about it. I know I want to live there for a long time to come, and this is the first time. I feel positive about everything. This has made me grow up and made me feel I should do everything to keep it nice.

I've had to work with people who I didn't like, I had to get on with them. I think I've learnt a hard lesson - you have to fight to get what you want in this life I think.

Irene

Tarzan

On the way to the baths, my son only three months old, this huge tree outside the baths caught my eye immediately. I thought umm, this looks like an interesting tree.

Then the kids get older, we all say hello to the tree every time we pass it, now it's our friend, part of the gang. When I go to the baths alone, I see it and say hello to the tree. Sometimes I hug it like we do when with the kids. I think all this, then later, I end up having a snooze in that tree – well - living in it. Tarzan's Tree !!!

The taxi firm nick-named me Tarzan.
'Go and pick Tarzan up, he's going out to the club.'

Yes, 'Tarzan' - why - because I lived in a tree.

Yes, a tree, a huge tree, maybe three hundred years old. A beech tree, my favourite tree, a beautiful tree.

Oh yes, a huge tree, big enough to sleep in.

First, I had to climb it - that took a wee while - anyhow, once up there, not frightened, let's have a snooze.

Very nice, but also a little scary - looking at the August night sky, cradled in the hands of a three hundred year old beech tree.

Yes, just a little over-whelming I'd say.

Advantages - no electricity bulbs, no phone bills, no poll tax, no neighbours. Well, there are some neighbours – squirrels - cheeky fast moving grey squirrels, flies, midges; but I can hear the owl across the way, and none of them playing too loud, none of the burglary and hey, I don't have to hoover or wash up.

What bliss!

Sean McAnespie

I live in a hostel, which helps people to adjust to normal life after all kinds of problems, ranging from having been injured to being involved in crime. What I think about now is very worrying - I have to avoid making my future home in areas where my attackers may still live. The police are not sure who attacked me.

In hospital it's difficult to distinguish one day from another. I had a head injury after being attacked. Special meals on Sundays were a landmark, and helped me to tell which day was which. On Mondays and Thursdays I go to Carter Bequest Hospital to learn how to read and speak again.

My Dad's Mum died in 1975. She had a room next to her kitchen. She had this room to eat in. She had seven children. One died at about six months old. The room was heated by a coal fire. There was no heating upstairs.

She had furniture which dated from before World War 2, probably from the 1930s. She wouldn't replace it. If she was given new things, she said 'Thank you' and put them away. My Dad and I visited her everyday when she was ill.

My future home would not necessarily be a big place. I'd like to try to make a bird-table. I'd like an allotment if I couldn't have a garden. This would be a means of people meeting one another, and sharing common interests.

I do my own cooking. I have to be careful about things in the oven, not to leave them too long.

I'd like a flat, maybe over a shop. A ground-floor flat would enable me to sit out in the sun but would be vulnerable to burglaries.

John

How The Hell Did That Happen?

As a child tucked up comfy and warm in my own bed, listening to rain lashed up against my window by the January gales, the last thing on my mind was the smelly 'TRAMP' I deliberately took a wide berth around earlier today.

Older, and now integrated into society without as much as ripple, I have passed this smelly "TRAMP" many times, my thoughts being 'Hope to God that never happens to me'.

Chancing on "Street People" always evokes mixed emotions. The youth sitting cross-legged, eyes fixed to the pavement, his polystyrene cup empty; the refugee eastern Bloc women, babe in arms, begging for bread; the smelly, alcohol-soaked old man asking for a smoke; and the Big Issue vendors.
So,
How much do you give and to whom?

Buskers -
Every time I see a particular one, I give a quid. Well - that's discrimination - why don't I give to the others? What makes some buskers so special? My favourite one is in Sheffield, ginger haired, ginger beard, biker type, with the cardboard sign exclaiming 'HOMELESS HUNGRY BUT HAPPY', banging out Dylan's *Like a Rolling Stone*. You see, even "street people" have marketing technique.

Until something happens to us, something that makes us see things as they really are, I think we all discriminate. I stopped when I became homeless. How the hell did that happen? Easy – first, fall out with the girlfriend; then into a self pity-full depression; sell your home; then indulge yourself basically, until the money runs out. THEN WHAT? Doss on mates' spare beds, settees, floors, until you piss'em off, then it's back to Mum's. That doesn't last long. Then it's time to sleep rough - under bridges, on park benches, woods, I even slept in a Beech Tree - oh, and the roof of a bandstand. Then you get wet, tired, smelly; in fact, people start to walk round you in the street and look the other way.

My Dad was an alcoholic. The worst enemy of an alkie is denial; once I accepted I was homeless, I began to help myself.

Pride has to go, before you can help your situation. Oh and fuck all those smug bastards who walk around you in the street LIKE I

USED TO. Then walk into TEESSIDE HOMELESS ACTION GROUP, 145 High Street, Redcar - Francis will be sat there with Ruby his dog, he gave me a number to ring, passed me their phone, within an hour I had a roof my head, 16 days later - my very own flat. Julie can sort your debt problems; Alison will gently navigate you through the mysterious world of computers, which is handy for CVs.

These good people still help me, and there are more people always on hand. My "HAPPENING" has changed me. It has helped me not to "DISCRIMINATE". However small your offering, give it unconditionally, it will land on fertile soil. Remember the ACORN!!!!!!!!

Sean McAnespie

The home was good; it felt like as if I could smell cakes cooking. Being happy in the home has made me a stronger person in myself, and having good neighbours has helped. I am happy.

I was in a sad home; I couldn't go out on my own because I felt that someone had dropped down, died. I was so unhappy and felt very unsafe. The home was on a corner of a roundabout. I felt very unsafe because there was a main road near by.

I would like to buy my own house and have an outside swimming pool; it would have a large garden and also have a big bedroom, big kitchen, a big lounge and also stairs leading upstairs and a hall. This is my dream house, it would feel more safe.

Marie

(these walls I once called home are now my trap)

Safe`

It starts again. The same each and every evening, but worse on Fridays. The walk up the stairs, in darkness, carrying my most precious belonging.

Here, the darkness holds no fears, no ghosts or ghouls hiding behind doors or lurking in corners to threaten me or my cargo. No, this darkness is warm and comforting. It can give me some hours of peace if I allow it, but usually, despite its soft embrace, it gives me apprehension enough to keep me alert and awake.

I suppose it's any father's story really. At least any father who loves his child above all else. Especially when I was so selfish before her birth and truly thought only of myself. Now I only think of her and how I hope to give her all I can. The best I have right now is my time and myself.

It's bedtime on Friday evening, when it's just Lauren and me. Pizzas are eaten along with cold glasses of milk to take away the spicy aftertaste of pepperoni. The bath is taken, with bubbles and toys, along with laughter. Radiator warm towels and pyjamas. Just in time we rush downstairs to watch her favourite programs, and I freely admit, mine also. Top of the Pops which is sung along to with gusto but little melody, followed by Fort Boyard - a game show which, while infantile and silly, is watched with awe and wonder. Occasionally a small voice pipes up, "Bet you could do that, dad," and it turns you into something more than just dad - actually a superman or worse, a clever cartoon character. But you don't really care, as you go along with your heroic poses and bad advice to the television teams who do not hear you. But Lauren does, and that's what matters most.

Nine o'clock arrives and little eyes become heavy, and slowly close. You dare not move yet. It's too soon, and despite the cramp in your left arm you hang on, completely still, until the breathing becomes soft, deep and regular. Slowly, oh so slowly, so not as disturb, you unfold your legs and ease the wrist of your left arm. Then with all the slow determination of a Tai Chi expert, you move carefully step by step out of the living room, into the hall and up the dark stairs. No lights are turned on, as this would awaken. But lights are not required in any case, due mainly to the number of times you've taken this exact same route. Ever so carefully Lauren is put to bed. Warm duvet to enclose and protect. Soft pillows for a lovely blonde head.

In the corner of her room is an old comfortable chair, usually covered in teddies and dolls. But every Friday I evict them to the floor at bath-time, as I know I will sit here, not in the room's darkest shadows, but in the room's natural light, so as not to startle if Lauren wakes. And thus begins the ritual. Is she breathing? Is she too hot or too cold? Are her dreams of happiness or does a nightmare linger where I cannot stop it causing distress? To sit here at this time is to face all your fears for a future that you cannot really predict. You want to be able to control an uncertain ageing from infant to adult.

You know that really you control nothing. If God, Buddha, Mohammed or others turn away their faces, then she is doomed. What the hell am I talking about doomed? No such thing - she is happy, cared for and loved beyond everything or anyone by both her parents. I would exchange life for her anytime, as would my lady.

At these moments I feel like a Samurai, not just sworn to protect, but waiting to protect. Or like an Arthurian knight dedicated to the quest. My goal is the safety and happiness of my child instead of a mythical realm. When she asks a question I want the answer; when she feels hunger, I look for "noodles and hot dogs". Kids do get some bizarre combinations. How do you protect someone from bad food advice? That's right advice. You advise them to eat well, brush their teeth, look both ways, eat slowly, chew more, don't gulp, you need sleep. Good God, isn't this just what your mother or father said to you? Did they go through this as well?

This need to always be there. To be there for emergencies or laughs. Laughs, this isn't funny. It's far too serious for laughs. Hold on, hold on. Take a deep breath, draft arse. God, it's always the same. Lauren sleeping happily, and me going rapidly insane. With a worry that at this moment does not exist.

It was never like this when I was a soldier. These anxieties for others, I just ignored them. That is, if I thought of them at all. I only cared about my task, never individuals or casualties. I was a rock where a sea of enemies were smashed. By skill, aggression and guile. Unfortunately, my colleague and friend also suffered, and died in my shadow. I was the strongest fortress of grey hard granite. Cold and aloof. Unbreachable, unconquerable, unforgiving. I was sentinel for my nation, my government, my queen. I offered my life without fear or regret, in the service of my country. Right or wrong, I accepted its gratitude with false humility, revelling in the glory, valour and fear. I, the sentinel of my people, was its bloody fist, driven into the enemies that were not enemies at all, and at my furious deadly heights a child, my child came into my life. Lauren.

So now I sit in the softest darkness and try to quell fears that I never had or felt. And the recognition in myself is that these real fears make me a better man. In fact, despite the childish baubles of victory which proclaimed me a man, I am more a man now when I walk down a lane or around a park holding Lauren's hand. All these fears are mine not Lauren's. Perhaps it's because I lived in the worst our world can offer, and now am blessed with the very best, that my confusion burns so brightly, why on a bath night I'll never know. I do know this, I wouldn't change anything.

Once I reach this stage of thoughts and memories on a Friday night, I start to calm down and relax. The past is the past, and no longer my present or future. I know my child is having a blinding time, and is loved by all she meets. I know she is happy, and so am I. I sit back in the old chair, relaxed. I am my child's sentinel, but a better one than just a warrior. I am a dad and a best buddy.

My eyes get heavy and without a thought blissful sleep arrives. Same every week. I wake up, slowly, gently, a warm breath on my cheek. "Hello, daddy," Lauren says. "You've been asleep and I've been looking after you."

Tony Bottrill

Houses

Bad house –
Barn, corrugated roof, two bed-roomed, next to river, middle of
nowhere, near railway viaduct, noisy nights, clatter, clatter. Open
fire. The one thing I detested was the water. Yellow like piss. When
having a bath once I had guests, small shrimp like things, some
dead, some not, in the yellow water. That was it - no more baths
there. Curiously no smell to the water, therefore VISUAL DISGUST!
Yellow piss-like water with shrimps in!!!!!!!!!.

Home –
Three bed-roomed terraced house, 3 storeys with paddy-field style
gardens, dropping down to running beck full of Rock Trout.
Everything about this house was perfect, especially Sunday. Sunday
dinner, smell of Sunday dinner, smell of the kids' hair drying after
bath time, noises of the kids and other kids pelting around the
rooms. In fact all the noises and smells were a joy, even the cars
passing out front sounded good, even, even fighting MAGPIES in
the beech tree out front sounded good. The songs from the brook,
the creaky back door, the cooing doves, the wind flowing through the
solitary sycamore and leylandii leaves. It sounded like some wise old
grandfather telling a story of olde. Yes, those Sounds and Smells.

Sean McAnespie

Home From Home

My father sensed that he was becoming ill. I wish I'd been able to help him more by not shouting demands. My Dad was a saintly person who used to be a proper Yorkshire iron and steel worker, slinger and grader. It's too late now. I missed showing him I have my own life.

Shortly before, and for a little time after his death, I was in Respite Care Home in Guisborough. One thing I liked about the home was 'young blood' - young nurses! They were looking for today, not yesterday. I had the feeling that they were giving me love. I can't say what love is, but love is there. I can sense the presence of love.

I missed going to the fridge like I do at home. I missed Darren and Tracy, my brother and his wife, telling me how much I was loved. In my own home they tell me that I am loved in both words and deeds. I missed looking at my photographs of my late Mam and Dad and other relatives.

My brother Darren is going to buy the house next door to his own, and will knock down the wall dividing it from his. I was born in Darren's present house.

This arrangement will provide me with self-contained quarters of my own but with help always near, for meals etc.

When future home was uncertain I was lost. Do I deserve love? Come back, my memories. Feelings of pain, life has begun again.

When I was in the Cheshire Home at Marske for Respite Care to give my Dad a break, the nurses were all female, they helped to bring me out of my shell. I disliked being taking to the toilet. I didn't mind for myself, but I felt embarrassed for the nurses' sake. I disliked the liver we were given for lunch. It looked like shoe soles. I couldn't eat it, but no alternative was offered.

I especially missed saying 'Goodnight' to my family.

Barry Welburn

My Mother Came To Stay

My Mother felt she had to live with my family and me because of her poor health, and inability to keep her house in perfect condition. She sold her home very cheaply to a housing association; it was a terraced house without a bathroom.

She arrived at our house in the passenger seat of a small removal van, with her caged budgie on her knee. My Mother shared our lives, whilst trying to maintain her independence. She made the bread and shared in the cooking.

Our semi-detached house was full - two double bedrooms, a single room and a bed sitting room - sleeping space for a family of five and Grandma.

Some of the time mother was happy; sometimes she was anxious and felt in the way - saying she was taking the space from the boys because they had to share.

As times changed, the children went to college, they got married, and my mother died. The house emptied, and now there is just my husband and me.

At first we felt sad, but now at times we guiltily enjoy the space.

Marjorie Parkinson

Dear Kitchen

Dear Kitchen,

Having a brilliant time away from you
I don't miss you at all.
I don't miss the pots
And clothes that always
Need washing
Or cleaning the floor
Or even the shopping
That needs putting away.
I won't see you soon.

Love Susan

Susan

I was upset when my ex-husband hit me a lot. I have been homeless six times and it hurt me. The house I live in makes me sad, but when I stay at Dave's house I am happy.

My house has a thin paper door and I have double sticky tape on the back doors to keep the draft out. The door is brown and thin and my heating bill is twenty-two pounds per week; it is a cold house. I am bored; I have no one to talk to and I hate being on my own. I have a lot of rubbish out at the back, but the girls play at a friend of mine's. We put the light on so the girls could play with the snow. They loved it so much, they can't wait until it snows again. A good house would make me happy, with friends to talk to, and a lovely garden, and to be near my friends and other people.

Sandra

My Relationship With My Flat

Sometimes my flat is my home,
It is my refuge, a four-roomed fort.
Sometimes however, it is my prison.
Besieged by youngsters, my hearts strings fraught.
Sometimes I cannot bear my flat,
Claustrophobic, I need to get out and breathe;
Other times, when the world has spat on me
I almost march there,
Unlock my door with relief.
Sometimes my window is my panorama,
But at night,
I can be scared to turn on a light.
Sometimes my window mirrors more than my reflection,
A man child,
Still juvenile
Yet at least his full height.

Garry Newmarch

I've been living on the streets for a year and three months. This is stressful, not getting no help off no-one or nowt. I've tried all sorts of organisations, but they didn't help because I was on drugs. People think you're going to pinch something off them.

Being on the street makes people ill mentally and physically. It's like a fight, you can win it or lose it. I know that people not involved with drugs get priority in being housed. I have a tent.

The only place that's helped us is the John Paul Centre. A catholic Father gave me his own shoes. See how new-looking and good quality they are. The Fathers are not allowed to give away money, but they can give goods. These clothes I'm wearing were given to me here.

All my money comes from begging – I'm lucky if I have a fiver a day, and it all goes into trying to get somewhere to live. See this leaflet? My only hope is in here – a Salvation Army Hostel has offered me a place at £8.60 per week. Yes, maybe I could get somewhere in Middlesbrough, but I want to get to this hostel in Newcastle, to get away from the local drugs scene. I'm trying to get far away from Middlesbrough. I've slept in Albert Park. This toast is the first food I've had in a long time.

Richard

On The Scrap Heap

Nothing in this room, belongs to me, why?
Familiar things, I can't identify,
It's a strange wardrobe, my clothes are within,
The prices are mounting, our budget is slim.
My son in a guest house, storage at high cost,
No meals provided; I'm completely lost;
Shared kitchen and toilet, I can't live like that,
Though my son is near me and that's a good start.
I hear noises of people walking about,
I'm in a panic, I've got to get out,
In the car, seat-belts on; please, lets go,
Where we'll finish up, we really don't know,
We need a home, a comfortable space,
Somewhere warm to hold us safe.

Ann Dulon

Dear Stranger

Dear Stranger,
        Help me get out of this house
        The walls are all wet with condensation
        The windowpanes are rotting
        The rooms are all damp
        Our rabbit has just been killed
        And the bedroom carpet is wet
        From the snow on the window ledge

Dear Stranger,
        Can you get me out of this house
        When the woman washes upstairs
        It comes through the ceiling
        And rains in the bedroom
        The kids kick footballs at the wall
        And give you loads of cheek
        When you tell them to go away
        Then they climb on the back garden wall
        And look in the window
        So we've covered it with margarine and lard

Dear Stranger,
        You don't know me but
        The walls of this place are threatening
        To crush my bones
        They plan to turn me into dust
        Nowhere is safe
        I am hiding in the cupboard under the stairs
        Talking to spiders that crawl
        Through my hair
        Soon I will be disappearing

Redcar and Cleveland MIND

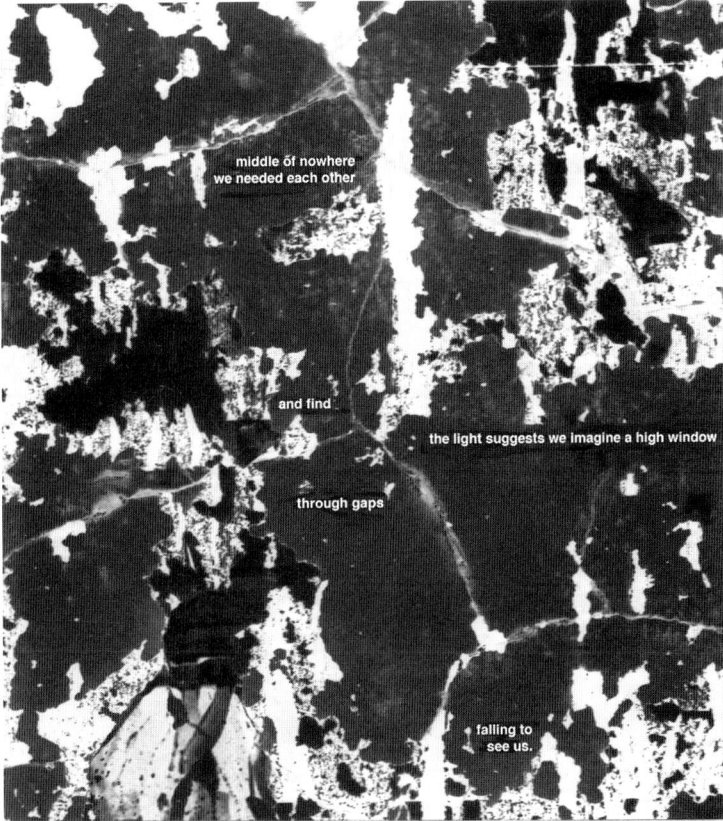

middle of nowhere
we needed each other

and find

the light suggests we imagine a high window

through gaps

falling to
see us.

The Moonlight on the Lake

Homesick, Homeless
Moonlight shines on the lake in Albert Park.
My home is not mine now.
The sky is heavy, and like me it's dark.

Homeless, Homesick
Stabs my heart sometimes,
Like a carving knife.

Home, Lord, Oh Lord,
Lord protect this refugee from life.
Feelings feel bad
Feel as if there is no more to say.

Bones are cold,
Bones feel so old
If my heart was still living, she could break
and this town, it's a stranger.
The lights are burning, but the streets are dark

Homeless, Homesick
and the moonlight shining
on the lake in Albert Park.

Garry Newmarch

Alone

Middle of nowhere
We needed each other
and find that day light
suggests
we imagine
a high window
through gaps
failing to see us.
We are part of darkness.
Seeping
into dreams,
Go home ghosts.

The Grange, Eston

Where Are My Things?

They say I'm a bit confused,
That I'm not safe to be alone in my own house,
So I've been assessed
And they say
I've agreed to go in to an old folks home.
Where are my things?

My house had six rooms, filled with my life,
Now I've got one bedroom
With my favourite chair
And two ornaments
And two pictures.
Where are my things?

I try my best,
I do as I'm asked,
I wash, I eat, I go to the toilet
And I go to bed when the time is right.
My thoughts
And my memories
Help me through the days.
But where are my things?

Marjorie Parkinson

Sealed Window

The children, returning from school
Find the house heavy with silence.
The clock stilled; curtains tight closed.
Accusatory dust coats every surface,
The carpet bears a mantel of stale crumbs.
The bathroom; a haven of bacterial smells,
Tells tales of neglect.

They listen, uncertain, outside the bedroom door.
Inside, she lies foetal curled tight
In some dark place.
Windows and doors firmly sealed
Barred from within.
The house had no memory; alzheimic, but
The children will always remember these shut down days.

Elizabeth Greathead

Not at Home

Aunty's clean house
Everything in its place
Pale pink carpet
Trampling mud in
Too clean
Not comfortable
Not daring to put a cup down
In case it marked somewhere.

Rooms with open doors into the dark
Who's here?
You cannot see
Not alone

Could be doors here
To be closed

Lena

He says He Loves me

He says he loves me
He didn't mean it
  I wouldn't do it if I didn't love you
He's going to get some help
He wouldn't have done it
If I'd done as I was told
  She just winds me up
  I'll never do it again
I can't leave I've got nowhere to go
I can't leave I've got nowhere to go
I can't leave I've got nowhere to go
  She's always nagging
I slipped and I fell
  She's just got to sort her act out
He's not that bad
Nobody else would want me anyway
I love him
  She's always looking at other blokes
  When we're out
The children need their dad
He's a really good dad
I can't cope on my own
  I'm so sorry, I promise to sort myself out
He's under a lot of stress at work
He's alright when he hasn't had a drink
  She knows I'm stressed when I've got no fags
No one understands him
He had a difficult childhood
He's alright most of the time
  I didn't hit her that HARD
I've got one of those faces that need to be smacked
  I NEVER BROKE HER FUCKING LEG!
I deserved it
  SHE SHOULDN'T HAVE HIT ME BACK!
He can't help getting angry

Cleveland Domestic Violence Forum

27

Lost 1978

What once was love had now become loathing
What had happened to the laughter and fun?
I don't know where it has all gone.
Children in their beds up stairs, warm and cosy and unaware,
Hidden away from the pain below,
No-one knew what was happening there –
In through the door he'd fall and stumble,
With more bottles in his hands,
Muttering, stuttering under his breath.
On the chair I'd sit with unease, I could not run,
I had nowhere to go.
No point in hiding, he would find me anyway.
Could not move, mouth tight shut,
Do not want to make a sound,
Not a word dare I speak, over to the chair he'd come,
Drunken breath pushed to my face
I know it won't be long until it's all over

Here it comes

Dragged up from my seat
Snarling and laughing in my face,
I dare not even look away
Arm raised high above his shoulder to make sure I didn't move
No point in ducking - he never missed.

Up against the wall he'd push me, lifted his fists, out they came
I would slide down to the floor, unable to move once more
Then out his foot came, just for good measure.
Up to bed he would stagger, won't be long till he's asleep.
Into the bathroom I would go, inspect the damage he'd done again,
I'd climb in bed beside the children, I knew he wouldn't come in there,
Could not go out for days and days, until the bruises had faded away.

Then one day I seemed to realise, this definitely could not go on,
I did not want the boys to see what their dad had done to me.

I packed our bags and in the night we left,
My family did not know what was happening in that house
They took us in and cared for us - a great relief.
In the chair I can relax, no more pain he can inflict,
Close your eyes

You can go to sleep.

Kathryn J.W.

Domestic

Doctor

Mrs Dawson again. She looks tired and pale. What a nervous woman she is.

How are you feeling today, Mrs.Dawon, still not sleeping?

I'd really like to get finished on time today.

So you're still very tired and a bit down. Have you got something on your mind?

She does look a bit of a mess. Her clothes are dirty.

Do you need more sleeping pills, Mrs.Dawson?

She says she's not getting on with her husband very well. What does she think I am - a bloody marriage guidance counsellor?

Could you and your husband maybe go to Relate? Maybe that would help.

I really do need to get home. I wanted to be there for Sam's birthday party.

OK, but maybe you could think about Relate. Talk to your husband about it. He seems to be a very understanding man. I'm sure he would go if you decide this is what you need.

I'm sure that she brings a lot of this on herself. If only she would talk to her husband. He seems such a caring man.

Well, maybe if you could manage to get some more sleep you would find that you are not so stressed and tired.

That seems to have done the trick, she seems happy with that.

OK, Mrs.Dawson, I'll give you another prescription for some sleeping pills.

Good. I might just make it in time to see Sam blow the candles out.

Mother

Called into Mother's today. Black eye. Really shaken up. He beat me again last night.

Mother's very good, very understanding. She says, she would rather I stayed for the children's sake. She believes the children should have their father. She tells me, leave if you want to, what ever you decide I'll stand by you. I'll help and support you. But don't you think you should stay until the children are older, she says, maybe things will get better.

She's got a friend, she says, who was in the same situation and she and her husband are getting on better than ever now.

Just look at me and your dad, she says, how long have we been married? Thirty years. We've had our ups and downs. She says, why, why, why, does this have to happen to our family?

Our Mary is so different, she says. She's happily married. She's got a lovely house she says, and a good job. Why can't you be more like our Mary she says.

Priest

Poor woman, so many problems, and not much of a life since she met him. She thought I was going to endorse society's view, that she should stay with him and hopefully sort it all out. I wonder if that's why not many women come to see me about the partner beating the hell out of them. I know it happens an awful lot, but they always seem to work it out for themselves.

I wonder what happened to Jenny Dawson. It must be about six months now since she came in here. Only her voice was recognisable, her face was in a terrible state. God above only knows what he'd done to the rest of her.

I've told her time and time again, that a husband is supposed to love and cherish his wife. Maybe they married in haste, but in this particular case she can't afford to repent at her leisure. I hope she got sorted out.

Wife

'Please, Tony, not again,' I said, 'I'm sorry, I forgot that you were home early.' He said, ' You fucking bitch, I expect my tea on the table when I get home'.
I saw that look in his eyes and I knew.
He grabbed my hair and twisted it, wrapped it several times around his hand and pulled it so hard I lost my balance.
'Owwww, no please, owww nooo,' I screamed at him. 'The kids, please, not in front of the kids.'
He said, 'Look you fucking little shit, you need to be taught a lesson.'
I screamed.
He pulled me by the hair and headed towards the stairs.
I tried to find my balance.
He finally got me to the bedroom and threw me on the bed.
The bastard took off his belt and started hitting me with it, he raised his fist and smacked it into my face.
When I came round, my face was sore and swollen. I had cuts all over my body and could hardly move.
I cried.
I looked up and my son was at the foot of the bed.
I sat up.
I said, 'OK, babe, are you hungry? Mammy will be down in five minutes, darling'.

Police

I've been called out to this Dawson woman at number thirteen.
Again. But when I get to the house everything's calmed down. Last time she said she was sorry for wasting my time.
We go away again.
I do feel sorry for her, but why does she stay there if that's going on? I know I couldn't.
He said last time I went that she takes medication to sleep, and that when she gets her period she goes mad. So, who do I believe?
The problem now for me is that I have this bloody D.V. form to fill out, and if I don't arrest him I'll have to say why.
So this time I will. I'll take him in even if I can't see any bruises on her.
She won't press charges.
So, we'll just have to keeping arresting him until she gives up messing everyone about.

Cleveland Domestic Violence Forum

Why Doesn't She Just Leave

Why does she keep going back
Why doesn't she just leave
Why does she put up with it
Why doesn't she hit him back
Why doesn't she tell him to fuck off

I wouldn't put up with it

We had no choice
We had to put up with it
We had no choice
People give up on marriage too easily these days
We had no choice
Everyone gets a slap now and again
We had no choice
We had no choice

You've made your bed so lie on it.

Cleveland Domestic Violence Forum

Blackbird

The clock tolls
Half past nine.
Only one drink left.
Pearls of sweat gather.
Outside the window
Daylight persists.
May, bringer of long days.
Outside the house a blackbird calls,
Welcoming the length of days.
Foraging.

Ten o'clock,
Pearls roll glistening.
Screams build behind my lips
Every second excruciates
Every nerve,
Every cell shrieks.

The blackbird sleeps little,
Sings early in spring.
From sunrise to sunset
Goes about the business of survival.
I do not sleep.
Sweating, shaking, hating
My life marked by
My ticking clock and the blackbird's song.

Morning breaks.
Sick with loathing,
I rise, stumbling
Through the debris
Of the previous night's
Desperate forage for sustenance.

Standing by the window watching.
I envy him his clean instincts,
His freedom;
He knows it,
His pale ringed eye pities me
In my prison.
I put my soul on his wings
My voice in his song.
Returning from the supermarket
I see him.
His wing, a stark black pyramid
Flutters in the gutter,
Is stilled.
Children will drop bricks on his corpse.

A sharp intake of breath
Glass on tarmac
Wine rains into gutter
And drain.
Sunlight on metal
Light dazzles.
One sharp impact
Darkness absorbs the light.
A heavier red stains
Gutter and drain.

Elizabeth Greathead

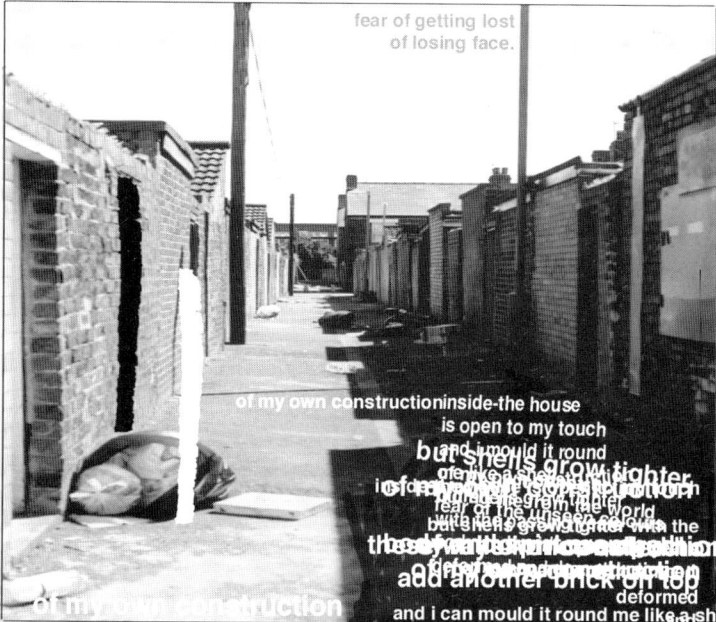

fear of getting lost
of losing face.

of my own constructioninside-the house
is open to my touch
and i mould it round
but shells grow tighter,

fear of the misery world

but shells grow tighter with the

and another brick on top
deformed
and i can mould it round me like a she

mole i should run

the shell is

of my own

construction.

The Hostel

The hostel fairy-tale
was mostly a lie.
There were witches all right,
served up fried
cooking fat.

The place was swarming
with lies.
Falling
just beyond her front tooth
the mute light
of the real world
hung by the thinnest
of cotton thread.

A fairy-tale morning
lying in pools,
colours shouted at
The thinnest mother;
slammed-tooth.

The Grange, Eston

Untitled

Through the bars a smoke-filled sky,
No sex, no drugs, no apple-pie,
As I lie sweating alone on my bed
An image of you flies round my head.

When heroin's the number one lust
You always hurt the ones who trust,
Lies, deceit, swear down on life,
Like the man says, 'It's my wife.'

It'll lead you past the garden path,
The jokes on you and it's no laugh,
You'll wind up in a concrete tomb,
In a smoke-filled, piss-stained, two-man room.

Pat Duffy

A Council Mausoleum

I can hear them
Talking, laughing, communing
With the television.
Black and white images: icons
Morecambe and Wise,
Friends of the family

The door opens,
My mother comes out
Goes into the kitchen, makes tea.
Places cups on a tray; stained
Blue earthenware. Comes back up the hall
Into the living room. The door closes.

There was no acknowledgement
No invitation for the watcher on the stairs.

I'm suspended in time
A ghost light
A projected image,
Imprisoned behind banister rails;
In a house that has long since
Crumbled to dust.

Outside the front door is a universe.
A constellation of possibilities.
I stand in its archway
Glancing back over my shoulder.
I never left;
Remaining loyal to the hope of finding love.

The house became my mother's womb
Where I waited for her to give me birth.

Elizabeth Greathead

Untitled

It all started off at 12 on the dot,
My birthday treat was a smoke of pot,
The local youth club was the venue –
Resin de cannabis was on the menu.

It was then I turned from bad to worse,
Nicking cash from the old girl's purse,
From black and blue to silver brown,
Life's a drain when you're really down.

Then me mother kicked me out,
With a tear in her eye as she clout as she shout,
Scurrying through streets night and day,
Scoring for money in ANY old way.

Then the keys turn and I'm holed in a cell,
No mother or brother or sister to tell,
No address, just my mess, was all I could give,
Banged up in a hostel is the space where I live.

Cooked up the river and swallowed the hook,
Chancing my skanking this Morpheus crook,
Yer black pinhole eyes leave nothing to chance,
My house is a mattress where I lance an a dance.

I wake to the bell,
Checking holes in my feet,
How I miss that dear mattress
On this bed called the street.

Michael McNicholas

Walls

These walls I once called home are now a trap,
Hiding me from the world, and it from me,
Fear of the unseen colours my perception,
Fear of getting lost, of losing face.

Inside - the house is open to my touch,
And I can mould it round me like a shell,
But shells grow tighter with the passing years,
Body and spirit cramped, deformed, and doomed.

Perhaps, like the sightless mole I should tunnel out?
The shell is, after all, my own construction.
Put out my hand for rescue, trust a stranger,
Or scuttle back inside and bar the door?
And add another brick a top the wall!

Chris Parkington

After kissing my Mum and brothers goodbye, we sat in the cab and drove towards the airport. My heart felt sad, leaving my loving family and friends behind, yet at the same time happy about starting a new life in England, with my husband and our daughter.

My husband and I had met in the October of 1995 - eighteen months later we got married in India. Since then we'd been coming to the UK every year to visit my husband's family. In a way I was preparing myself for the idea of coming to live in England. When we got married it was understood that I would have to move to England with my husband, and we migrated here in June 2000.

In the beginning life in England was very different from what I was used to in India. I found it was very difficult to adjust myself to the new culture. Visiting on holiday was very different from actually coming to live here. I found the place very quiet and haunted, compared to the hustle and bustle of city life in Bombay, where I came from. I was very scared to stay on my own in the house, while my husband went to work. I could hear the clock ticking, the fridge humming, the tap dripping and the heater buzzing. I felt like the house was haunted too

It was supposed to be summer, but the sky was always oozing with thick black clouds. I hardly ever saw the sun in its full splendour and glory. It was always wet and dull and grey - the cold was unbearable. I couldn't imagine going out of the house without layers and layers of clothing. The fire was on twenty-four hours a day, seven days a week, which made me sleepy all the time. The food was very bland, which made me constipated. I had to sprinkle all my spices over the food before eating it. The shower and the toilet had its own story…..

I began to miss home very badly. I missed the bright sunny days, my family and friends. I especially missed the noise and hustle and bustle around me.

A year down the line, things have changed. The house doesn't feel haunted anymore, I've got used to the strange and funny noises. I found the shop where they sell Asian goods, so I can cook Indian food. I have got used to the weather - sunshine or no sunshine - life goes on; yet a bright sunny sky brings life into a dull day. I'm used to the showers and toilet. I have become acclimatised, too.

I can say that I'm adjusted to the English culture and climate. My in-laws made life a bit easier for me, helping me adjust to the new

environment. The people are very supportive, friendly and helpful. I made lots of Asian and English friends. I feel at home, yet I miss home – miss people, colleagues, the climate, the busy life of a city. It is like "Home and Away". I am at home, yet at the same time miles and miles away from home.
   "HOME SWEET HOME".

Nirmala Harris

My name is Asal, I am 30 years old, I come from Tehran in Iran. In spite of the fact that I had many problems in my country, I was hopeful about the future. All my hope is my only son.

Everything sounded different when I entered the UK. We were placed in a hotel at the beginning of our arrival.

Although I was in great pain, I tried to soothe myself. I and my son were transferred to Middlesbrough after 7 days. I started weeping when I settled in the new house. I still remember how the walls and the doors of the accommodation were queer to me. I liked to shout at the time, because I didn't know anybody.

I wished to have a power to destroy everything. I liked to tell everybody in the world, " I am a human being, I'm a woman, a lonely woman". Now, I'm putting all my efforts into bringing up my son.

Whenever I look to the past, I remember my mother's smile.

Sometimes, I find myself as a baby at the breast of its mother. Yes, I still remember my mother's look. Although I am far away from her, I never forget what she said about the difference between right and wrong.

Asal

it starts again, the same
each and every evening,
but worse on fridays.

My name is Maryam. I'm thirty-one years old. I got divorced in Iran. Now I'm living with my daughter, Anahita. Because of the religious rules, women have to wear a scarf, to hide their whole body, and put on a veil when they go out. In my country, women also enjoy fewer civil rights than men; for instance, they can't get a divorce, even in the worst conditions, if their husbands don't want them to.

I think women have equal rights to men in the UK. That is why I'm very pleased.

I was an accountant in my country, Iran. I worked in the Medical Sciences University Department of Accountancy. But here, I have a lot of spare time. I couldn't attend a full time English course, because I was too late to enrol. Consequently, most of the time I'm without any engagements, which really does concern me.

Sometimes, I'm quite depressed about such circumstances. In my view, if we had recreational facilities, like sports, our spirits would be less troubled.

Maryam

I'm Said, I came from Iran in 2000. I managed to get myself to Gatwick (UK), though with a lot of problems. On my arrival I found out that English people are very kind.

After a while, I was transferred from Gatwick to Middlesbrough. Currently I benefit from the facilities of accommodation, income and a good education.

After waiting one and a half years, my claim was finally refused for unknown reasons. I appealed to the court against the refusal, but still I'm waiting for a reply. As I see it, the law in this land operates at a very slow pace. I wish to find peace and freedom in my country and return there very soon.

Here, continues to feel like a jail to me, but with the doors held open by a humane jailer.

Said

News From Home

Alone, and a cold wind blowing
In dusty British streets
With pasty British faces
And nothing, no-one known
And speaking/signing Martians
And nowhere with a smile
And hours to kill till bedtime
And only time to spend
And news from home/ no news from home
And news from home/ no news from home
And who's to say which is the best

And an unfamiliar skyline
And unfamiliar earth
And nowhere any comfort
And nowhere any ease –

And were you right to do it
And had you any choice
And can you make a life here
And can you move your heart
With ruins back behind you
And rubble all around
And grit instead of honey
And scratch and shame to wear
And news from home/ no news from home
And news from home/ no news from home
And who's to say which is the best
And who's to say
And who's to help

And you try to build a bunker
To house your shattered soul
To glue concrete confetti
To the outline of a man

You feel slightly less a person
And slightly less alive
And what you need to feel is
And what you need
To feel
Is
Slightly less alone
Slightly less
Alone,
With a cold wind blowing.

Anon

My name is Soheila. I came from Masyed Solayman in Iran. I am 27 years old. I find many things interesting in UK. Women are living with ease, they are not working hard. Most of them purchase ready foods from shops – in Iran women spend the greatest part of their lives in the kitchen.

Women's clothing is another issue in my country, but here, women are quite free to wear or select different clothes. They are not obliged to cover their whole bodies, or to be beneath the veil

Climate, of-course, varies from country to country. The weather is almost monotonous here. It is often wet and cold. There are some seasons that seem to last for two short months or four long months in the UK, whereas all seasons are three months in Iran.

There is also a big difference between the schools of the two countries. In my country, boys and girls are educated in separate schools. They have to obey the restrictive rules of these educational centres. Students have to participate in governmental rallies and demonstrations, and to appear to tolerate the rigid regulations of such systems.

School are not free in Iran as they are in UK. Parents have to pay all funds and fees, which are claimed by Headteachers, yet they don't give any food to poor children at schools!

Soheila

Don't Shoot at the Corpse

How did he come to find himself in Middlesbrough? He did not ask this question any more. He was there, and he couldn't say that fate had spoiled him. Was he lucky or unlucky? Difficult to answer. He had escaped the massacres of the civil war, but there had been two years without any news from his family. Were they still alive? His father, his mother, his brothers and sisters, scattered in the rebel attack on the village. Had they survived the carnage? Are they somewhere? Can he join them?

Why did he find himself alone, on the other side of the world?

But here he was, in this state of mind – he would have to forge a new life. The town was full of people, but he did not see anybody. When he scrutinised the faces, it was to try to recognise someone – sometimes his mother, sometimes his brother, before he would realise that, unfortunately, he was the victim of hallucinations. He was roaming the streets the whole day, his head low, shoulders stooped, in the rain, in the sun, looking for nothing, his soul lost in the forests around his village, as he recalled the daily scenes with his family and friends; the joys of the harvest after months of labour in the fields; the triumphal return from a day's hunting in the heart of the forest; the animated evenings of chit-chat around the fire; the musical groups and the dancing; the hot meals served daily by his mother.

Ah, the hot meals that his mother served, will he taste them again one day? He had burned his tongue a thousand and one times being impatient – they were so good – before the mocking smile of the famous cook.

She was a magician who made works of art out of nothing, in her kitchen. Like the day she succeeded in making a dish based on pistachio, when there was no more pistachio. It was always a joy to see her at work, to see the ease with which she manipulated her condiments, juggled the frying pans, and judged the compositions in more than four pots at a time, and used magic to free herself from the children who blocked the entrance to the kitchen, pretending to be hungry to make meal time come all the sooner. And they would smile at each other, when they saw their father making unexplained and unnecessary visits – the aroma that preceded the meals would spill outside, and was always enough to make people lose their dignity.

He was smiling, even today, remembering all this, but here in Middlesbrough his smile did not have the same warmth; it was no more than a bitter stimulation in the corner of his lips, the smile of a man conscious of his uselessness.

To forget?

But what would fill his head then?

All the time he would be asking himself how to replace the happiness that he had known, back in his village. He lifted his head and looked around him. He had walked to the park with zombie steps, and found himself seated. How long had he been there, and did it matter? Ten minutes or two hours – what difference did it make? For months the days had passed, each resembling each other, but each one wrapping him in more and more layers of sadness.

Not far from him, on the other side of the bench, a respectable lady had a very passionate conversation with her Pekinese. On the path walked an arrogant gentleman, proudly showing off his pair of dogs – actually the park was saturated with people playing 'go fetch' with their dogs. Was this his new life; a world where everybody has his dog, his cat or maybe both? No, not to have friends, no greetings on the street; to have a dog, to talk only to your dog or possibly the dogs of others.

It was this, his new life; to live in a street with seventy doors, never to have seen a single one open. To whom could he speak about the sun? To whom could he speak about the rain? For whom could he describe the song of the forest birds in the early mornings? To whom could he say what it was like to track a lion, or confront a buffalo? To whom could he explain the feeling of escaping a herd of killer gorillas? To no-one. By day and by night the street was empty, shy, gloomy . The neighbours who made so much noise on the other side of the wall, wore a funeral mask once in the street.

It was another world.

A different world, different customs, people from another planet, too far from his Africa, too difficult to understand. He did try at the beginning, but he couldn't do it. He did not know how to live like them.

To forget?

But what would fill his head then?

Nothing, realising this every time he asked the question.

Nothing……..

The sun was setting bit by bit, the currents of air were charged with humidity, the park was starting to empty. He stood up with difficulty, with regret, and chose a path at random, without really hoping that it would lead straight to the exit.

The lady with the Pekinese stared at him indifferently for a short moment, before rejoining her companion. It was this, his new life, without friends, without family, nothing to live for but memories, and his label – 'Asylum Seeker'.

Bernard Petegou

My name is Leila, I am from Shiraz in Iran. I have been in Redcar for seven months. I am 31 years old.

Here, many things look interesting to me. For instance, pigeons and some other birds are easily coming into view at town centre, and squirrels are quite free to climb or go down the trees.

Unfortunately, in Iran, children have not been instructed how to behave towards animals, especially the birds. If a teenage child finds a rabbit or any animal, he will set a trap to catch it.

Health care also differs from what I see in UK. Here, to send an ambulance takes a short time, and it is free, while that is not so in my country. Wholly, the British people are in agreement with all civil liberties, yet the same rights are being considered as crime in Iran.

For example, the Government don't allow the men and boys to put in an earring, to have long hair, or to make friendship with women and girls. Moreover, the women and girls are not allowed to walk with men and boys, or to take some positions, such as judgement.

More interesting is that both sexes are obliged not to wear casual clothes, not to watch any sexy film, not to listen to songs and any western music, or to change their religion and so on.

Leila

I did it.
I open the gate.

All this way by my self.

I am from Iran. I was born in 1969. I came with my two sons in July 2000. I was in London at first.

I'll always remember when I arrived in Middlesbrough, it was foggy weather. From that first view, I grasped that such a scene illustrated a deep gloom over this town, and on me, myself, too. What a bad day it was!

I wept a lot. Everything was terrible. The rooms were full of dust, the village (Grangetown) quite quiet, and the people all strangers. Many times I have seen how the neighbours and some children attacked me and my poor kids, how they knocked on the door in a very wild manner, how they broke the windows, and how they assaulted my sons.

In spite of what happened to me, I like most of the people of this country. I believe there are both good and bad everywhere. In London, I was never faced with these problems.

It's momentous to say that in general, women in the UK have equal rights to men.

M. Piroozi

My name is Neda. I'm 26 years old. I came from Iran in February 2001. I have lived in Middlesbrough for four months. I had a lot of problems during my journey.

Here, I admire the liveliness of elderly people, and the priority of women in getting important jobs. To my mind, women's clothing here is quite different from what is current in Iran.

In my country we have to cover the whole of our bodies, even if the temperature is over 50 degrees Centigrade in the summer. If a woman smokes, she will lose her dignity.

The government ignores the concerns of the female sex, and what they say they will do for women, they do for appearance, rather than in practice.

Neda

Arrival

In huge silver planes and crowded boats,
We crossed from hot to cold,
Our suitcases crammed with unsuitable clothes
And ornaments and photos of
Everyone and everywhere,
And texts from the Koran
And fearful good wishes
And kisses from our mothers,
And we always thought we would return –
And we always thought we would return
To find ourselves and the land unchanged.
We unpacked the picture frames
And read the holy verses
And tried to keep the old country ways;
And we got up early for the post from home,
Where we knew everything
Would be the same,
And we would be the same
When we returned;
And our children were born
In boomtown Middlesbrough,
And our lives settled,
And the streets and the shops
And the faces became familiar,
And we polished the pictures
In which everything was still the same,
And we took our British-Asian children
Visiting to Pakistan,
Home for grandmothers' kisses,
And it didn't feel the same,
Not at all.

Back in Middlesbrough,
More children were born
And some people died,
And the ceremonies were in our houses,
And all these happenings
Make a home your home.

Our roots have stretched very far,
And our children will be the flowers
That travel further.

Ojalah group

Home is a place where your heart and soul and spirit and mind feel fed and at peace - in harmony - you're not having to protect yourself or put up a front, and you're not having to be someone whom somebody else wants you to be.

Disabled people are a bit like royalty - the whole of who you are is vetted through someone else. You can't lose your temper. You can't express normal human emotions without them being vetted by someone else.

Your whole being is filtered by someone else.

Avril Harris

Does your mother work?

My Mother had a strict routine:- each day had a certain job.

Washing on Monday
Ironing on Tuesday
Living room and kitchen on Wednesday
Bedrooms on Thursday
Shopping on Friday

My mother could not let her standards drop. When I married and had a family to look after, I felt I must keep the standards up or the house would disintegrate. Later I realised I could relax these standards and have a part time job and activities with the family.

Does your mother work? - My Mother always asked my new friends. She felt inferior, because she had to work to make ends meet.

Does your Mother work? - I ask my daughter's new friends, because I feel inferior, because I don't work, and stay at home and look after the family.

Marjorie Parkinson

Edna Davies

I always felt I had to take a back seat in the family, because of my disability.

I went into the orthopaedic hospital at Kirby Moorside when I was two. They only let the parents visit once a month, and I can remember my mother crying, because I didn't recognise her.

I felt at home in the hospital, everyone had their own difficulties. At Marton Grove School some of the children were cruel. One day, I had my arm in a plaster cast, and I belted a girl right across the head for calling me peg leg. It was all right, though, because her mother took my side, and I felt much better for it.

Then I went away, right down to Exeter, to the Rehabilitation Centre. It took ages on the train, I was jiggered when I got there. We had some fun there. I had a page boy hair style and two lovely slides, but the men there used to tease me and plait my hair. It was quite flattering, but I was always having to tidy up at lunch time. It was all in good fun, though.

After my mother died, there was just my father and me at home. We shared a taste in food, so I told him what he had to get and we both cooked it. But when he died, the social services said I wasn't safe, with the epilepsy. I feel a funny tingling in my legs and then it hits the top of my head. Anyway, I went into Blenheim House in Thornaby.

Some of the staff there used to try to make your mind up for you. They thought if you were disabled, you must be stupid as well. I used to say, I've still got a brain, you know. I had a room next door to a man with a crab-apple face. He used to ask me to turn the radio down, so I pretended I was stupid, and I turned it up instead.

Then a social worker suggested to me that I could live in sheltered accommodation. When I moved, the staff said, "We'll come and visit you", but I said, "I'm only going to get away from you lot!"

So now I live in my little bungalow, and I've got two care workers who come and help me, and the warden to keep an eye, and I wear a personal buzzer, straight to her house.

I can play my tapes - sometimes it's musicals, some days I go Country and Western, some days I come over all Mozart. I can watch what I want on the telly, but sometimes it's a load of rubbish, so I listen to radio Cleveland.

Everything I've got in my house all belongs to me. The warden took me shopping so I could choose for myself.

I don't get out too much, I tried an old persons' day centre, but I thought it was boring - I could stay at home and go to sleep in comfort, if I just wanted to do that.

I've had physical difficulties to deal with all my life, but I've still got all my marbles and I feel better off than Princess Margaret, having to be pushed about. I'm happy to remember my brother, we used to jitterbug and he used to slide me on the floor and pick me up and pretend to throw me in the air.

Once, a boy on the estate, about nine or ten, walked behind me, copying my walk, to make fun of me. I turned round and said, "Do you know, son, when you're as old as me, you might walk like me; or on the other hand, you might be six feet under."

His face went bright red. Now, when I see him, he offers to carry my bag, and he helps me.

We keep hearing about bogus callers on the estate, which is a bit upsetting, but in general I feel peaceful and content here.

Edna Davies

Home

A refuge, a cage or a trap?
Home was a place I came back to - to eat, to sleep, and to prepare for the next day. But home was not a trap. I could leave whenever I wanted to.

Now - I must plan it like a military campaign.
Now - I have to say where I'm going, and with whom.
Now - I am restricted to places I have been trained to move about in.
Now - I must be accompanied everywhere else.

And what crime have I committed that my freedom is thus curtailed?
I have lost my sight!

Indoors I move freely from room to room, the contents of each being my signposts. Door-posts, tables, work-surfaces, boxes - they are my map, and woe betide anyone who moves any of them!
Every new addition is a potential hazard: a pair of shoes by the front door; shopping left in the kitchen; a cat on the stairs.
Even the items I know can prove dangerous. Is this a bottle of squash or of cleaning fluid? Am I opening a can of stew or of cat food? Is the gas alight on the hob, or has it blown out? Is this one of my pills or just a sweet that got dropped?
At the front door, is it really the meter reader?, the milkman?, the postman?
No wonder the only place I feel safe is in bed! Tucked up tight, with my teddy bear!

Chris Parkington

could be

doors here, to be closed

I'm in a Care home for a week: Blenheim House, Thornaby. It's a lovely place and lovely people. I get a break from my brothers. That's what brothers do, isn't it? Get on your nerves! Sometimes I wish I had a sister.

I like the atmosphere of the home. It's friendly. The meals are lovely. Anything you need, the staff will just do it for you. I enjoy the peace and quiet. My family home is noisy.

I don't like to rely on people. I like to do things myself if I can. I have a bit more freedom at Blenheim House as the staff are strangers, but at home I have to consider the feeling of my family, who are emotionally involved with me.

My ideal home would have to have suited to my taste. First of all, it would have to be bright, but to have dimmer lights to suit the way I was feeling.

I like our present home because it's bigger than the last one. This is a good thing for my wheelchair and I have more space to do my exercises. I   love doing exercises.

Music makes me happy - all kinds except opera.

I have my own room downstairs though I sleep upstairs, with Sky, Satellite TV, video recorder, tapes etc. The room upstairs is for sleeping only. I can have a bit of quiet in my own hobby room downstairs. My downstairs toilet and bathroom and shower were all built for me in a special extension. I feel private there.

There are patio doors in the garden wide enough for my wheelchair.

My Nana's house was very small and very homely. I liked the living room because the furniture was close together which made it easy. Nana had her own special chair. It was leather - I think, brown. Nana always gave sweets or money to my brother and me.

The house had a yard and a shed and, I think, a little wall. The grass was very tall I seem to remember. I thought there were animals, frogs and worms, hidden in the grass. I like frogs.

Nana had a special toilet because she couldn't walk very well. When Nana died it felt awkward in the house. I was told that one night she collapsed suddenly on the landing and she died soon afterwards.

My surviving Nana has a small house in Central Middlesbrough. I like the dining-hall. The last time I went it had a table-cloth. It was purple. I liked the colour especially, I like violet colours. There were chairs around the table. They were tall chairs - wooden. I liked their shape and their dark brown colour. I liked the living room because the furniture was close together. This made it cosy. I liked the very old furniture.

I've been to Nana's house once or twice. Sometimes I get worried because she's getting old. She smokes a bit and has a bad chest. She has to use an inhaler. I've already lost two Nanas. Her present house is bad for her, she needs a bungalow.

I once went to look at a Home for people in wheelchairs and who have other disabilities. It felt uncomfortable. It wasn't t very homely. There were awkward feelings in the atmosphere. I decided not to live or stay there. It *was* too big. I was afraid I might get lost. There were too few staff from what I could see. I might be wrong, but that's what I felt.

I know that my family love me – that's what makes my usual home special.

Lisa Dalton

Plastic

Home again and the familiar smell of plastic,
Mum cooking tea,
Bacon and eggs again.
The smell runs through the house to meet me at the door;
I can smell after-shave on my dad.
He's going down the pub again.
Father, mother, love.
I am aged five.
I can smell the bubble-bath,
The damp wood burning in the fire,
The smoke running up the chimney.
It is night-time,
Time with my mother,
A happy time before bed,
Sitting on the sofa in the front room
Watching TV
With an open fire,
While my dad is in the pub.
Sitting with my head on her lap,
The smell of plastic on her clothes.
A time of joy,
My mother caresses my head as I sleep
And starts to weep.

Sean

A Breeze on the Wing

Lying in my prison cell
Wondering what I've done wrong,
Wishing that I was at work
With family where I belong,

But this is where I have to stay,
With the cons and with the screws,
Listening to the lonely echoes
Of the prisoners on the twos.

Then the silence stills the halls
Followed by a breeze,
It's then you hear the horrible voices
Of the prisoners on the threes.

I then go back to being alone,
Sheltering from my fears,
Trying to cry, to help myself,
But the breeze holds back my tears.

The pain it just won't leave me,
But for my family I must be strong,
And think of all the good times ahead,
When I'm home, where I belong.

Paddy Mcgrath

Tiobraid Arann

Tipperary's in my mind,
It's like an emerald beam,
Until I hear the door unlock
And it wakes me from my dream.

Dreams are all that I have left,
And shouldn't be misplaced,
I cannot blank them from my mind
Cos dreams are not to waste.

I try to dream a dream of home,
So I can feel secure,
But prison nightmares haunt my mind
And the scars are left too sore.

I hope you know just how I feel
When my dreams they don't come true,
But if I dream the same old dreams
Perhaps they'll see me through.

Christie McGrath

Untitled

To me home's alone
To me
Cold means warm heat means
Hate irate
I'm a law breaker
Scared paranoid lustful
Love to bust the horror with me frightnin lightning
Me biggest ambition is to have one
Sex is pinky ointment
Rub it into, probs no rocks
Just blocks my childhood expulsion
Rejection repulsion

Needles and misses and drug swap pisses
Rattle brown down in a love red mist
I see my fear

Rattle me: see the yellow pus filled mustard
Tomorrow is white and crisp
Can you taste it, brother?
It tastes like shit
Like scabby bacon and tuna Sundays
It's dog meat turkey crusty edges
Hedges the bets that the coppers
Have spat on the rest

My future is tasteless, uncertain
Like a drink of bitter air
You metamorphose
Into a rat
Greedy infectious ugly rat
Two faced – I'll sting you behind yer back
And climb on clucking
Like a turkey pleading with Christmas to take him home.

Mark Tyler

Homeless Life

The hill's too steep, but you say
You would like to see me climb it.

I live in a freedom jail

Fired from your aggression pistol
Drugs crack my schizophrenic back
I'm an unfaithful lover in my barred pit
I taste rejection the size of an oil rig leg
It throws me out the door
To score.

My home,
The whore-house of stinking nappies
Varicose veined alleys
Typhoid slinks and scally rallies
My home a sickly bile spew
My days are smack brown
My home town manacles my body down
A celebration drink of green
That shows my future where I've been
I bite and taste this peach juice red

As I stand staring at you
With my past glaring at you
Like the flame from the yard
Where you stole my pride
On that journey
You made my rattlin bones ride

Sleeping
I float into a dolphin's skin

Ted Hanley

every thing
sounded different

Holme House Hell

I sit and think and I wonder why,
I've wasted my life, I begin to cry;
A tortured past and shattered dreams,
A drunken father and mother's screams.
Growing up was so hard to bear,
Divorce is cruel, they do not care.
Single parent with no money to cope,
My mother tried but without any hope.
Sent to school in nothing but rags,
Couldn't have a uniform - she needed her fags.
Sugar bread sandwich no Sunday dinner,
For a growing child I was getting thinner;
Bullied at school and abused at home,
It wasn't long before I started to roam.
A new found freedom out on the streets,
I had to survive, I started stealing sweets.
Aged only twelve committing crime,
Empty houses, I was just killing time.
It wasn't long before I got caught,
I finally got the attention I sought.
This went on for another three years,
Then I was sent to prison aged fifteen years.
I sit here now in my Holme House cell,
I haven't escaped this is still like hell.
I look out my window, up at the stars,
That's all I can do behind these bars,
I pace my floor with a wide eyed stare,
Why is my life so empty and bare?
I look in my mirror and what do I see,
Yes, that's right, it's no longer me.
I can't stop thinking and wondering why,
I am thirty-two and I still cry.

Alan Dent

Holme Sweet Holme

As daylight turns to nightfall,
And the evenings they grow lame,
I go behind the metal door
Like a wind behind a flame.

It's there I spend a lonely night
Until the break of day,
Though nothing ever seems to change
I still have time to pray.

I pray to walk out on my own
Not under lock and key,
I guess I'm not the only one
There's many more like me.

I want to be a human being,
And not just left to slumber,
To get put of this bingo-box
And be more than a number.

And when I see the grass of home
Where beer is on the rack,
I'll walk towards a happy life
And swear I won't look back.

Christie McGrath

Holme House Hotel

A unique opportunity to visit this once-in-a-lifetime time-share accommodation. Holme House Hotel has everything you could wish to make your stay a pleasant one :-

- An outstanding range of fitness and health facilities
- The best food in the North East
- Fantastic view from all the bedrooms of rolling green hills and countryside
- TV with video at week-ends
- The latest in full security systems
- Easy access to the A19

On arrival you will be greeted by our friendly and attentive staff who will do their best to make your stay an enjoyable and memorable one.

Holme Hotel is an up-to date, fully modern hotel, with *en suite* bedrooms and showers and toilets on all landings.

Our first-class medical facilities cater for all minor and major injuries, from broken fingernails to bruised egos.

Sit back and relax, as our highly trained and enthusiastic staff show you how to have a really good time.

Try our distinctive Holme House wardrobe, designed to make you stand out in a crowd.

Sample the gastronomic pleasure of the *a la carte* gourmet food, cooked by our Michelin 2-star chefs, and served by our highly-trained staff. Full English breakfast (including the traditional lumpy porridge) is served at 7.30am. Visitors are especially urged to try our famous fillet of tyre-track.

Join your fellow guests in the evenings for indoor games, including pool, table tennis, table football, pool, table-tennis, table football......

Holme House Hotel - the experience of a lifetime - home from home - regular guests come back year after year.

Can you afford **not** to visit Holme House?

Houseblock 3 Creative Writing Group, HMP Holme House

Arrival

I touched a tree today. Walked right up to it and grasped the gnarled, mossy bark in both hands. To see what it felt like. No trees in Strangeways, though I once saw a sycamore seedling which had taken root in a gully: brave, sprouting a hopeful leaf. Until someone kicked it.

But this was an aged, rambling oak. I felt the bark for a minute, then let go, because my eyes were watering. The breeze, I think. I reminded myself that it'll still be there tomorrow.

I'd dreamed of Yorkshire for 1,325 nights and at last, there it was. For all its moods, I've never seen it look quite as lovely. Dropping down from the dark hills above Colne, the prison 'bus lurched around the tightening corners. Outside, the Lancashire moors gave way to gentler slopes, the wind-bent trees straightening all the while, greener and greener. Spring lambs skipping around on thick, wobbly legs. Millstone grit cottages and corner shops.

I'd been warned. "Freedom's hard to get used to," they'd said.

It hit me in Reception. Sunlight streamed through the open doorway, the breeze rustling through the trees on the other side of the fence. I could see life again; traffic flashing past along the road. Houses - semi detached ordinariness, where kids play on trimmed lawns, women hang out washing in the April breeze, and cats curl up on sun-warmed doorsteps.

The governor saw us all, in the old house. We sat in a carpeted room and she spoke - and listened. She asked if any of us had experienced any problems. I had, getting off the bus, and told her so, blushing, feeling bloody stupid, in front of the others. They'd all come from Cat C's. "That's the damage that's been done to you," she said; then added, " The damage we're going to put right, here."

I ate that evening in a carpeted, wallpapered dining room, eating proper food with stainless steel cutlery off a china plate on a smart table. Afterwards, I took a stroll around the grounds, taking in the spring sunshine. I know I should have been happy, but the words kept coming back to me - 'the damage.' Irrational, crippling panic set in. Can they put it right? Because for the life of me, it didn't feel like it.

I walked around the fence, listening to the birds singing, the cars passing by. Like a limb numbed by inactivity, the relief is welcome. But it's tempered by pain, as the blood rushes to long-forgotten corners of a concrete-walled, Cat 'B' mind.

It felt strange, sleeping in a room with a wooden door which is unlocked all night. I'd wake, then pad quietly over to it and try the handle, just to see that it still opened and that it hadn't all just been a dream. So many people had told me the same thing - the freedom's hard to get used to. As if they actually missed being locked up.

But that's not it at all. It's this: I'd become conditioned to being locked up. When I left my room in the small hours, to go to the toilet, I opened the door slowly, carefully, then trod gingerly on the edge of slippered feet, making no sound; scared to death of being where I shouldn't be.

When I was a kid I kept a rabbit in a hutch. One day in the summer holidays whilst playing in the garden, I opened the door to let it run around. It cowered in a corner.

I know how it felt.

This place is no holiday camp. Liken it to a convalescent home if you will, where the inmates don't even realise they need to convalesce until they arrive.

It's a place of contrasts, where conditioned, demoralised wrecks rub shoulders with the almost-healed; their lives already beginning to slot into place. Feelings of envy and admiration.

And hope, at last.

Keith Rigby

Coming up from the Beach

Up the ash bank to the top of the beach banks,
Which way to go?
The shortcut to the pit compound,
Or the scenic route over the top of the banks?
It's creepy in the dark,
Trees all around,
Crab-apple trees, flowers, nut trees,
The smell of sewage from the dene,
Diesel engines.
The cry of seagulls, crows, kestrels in flight,
The fence around the pit compound, grey, steel, spiked,
Dutt heaps, plumes of smoke from JCBs in the compound,
The conveyor belt,
Fisherman on the shore,
Acidic smells of burning plastic and copper wire.
Going home for my tea.
I still haven't decided which way to go;
It's getting darker and I turn around,
The white of the waves crashing on the shore.
Farther out, the sea is like a sheet of black, rippling glass
And on the horizon a golden red shimmering of a setting sun.
I take the short-cut home,
Past the compound and its forlorn-looking steel spiked fence,
Up by the allotments.
I can smell pigeons-lofts, rabbit hutches, creosoted fences.
I am at the bridge below the train tracks.
The train stands there with its convoy of grey metal tubs,
The dusty smell of coal and oil.
Through the bridge and up the cobble-stoned pavement.
Nearly home,
In at the first of the eleven rows of houses,
The pit wall looming above me.
The smell of the smoke from the coal fire chimneys
The almost ominous orange light cast from the street-lights.
I'm at the bottom of the street now,
Turning the corner, up the road to number 9.
Outside the green gate, the paint flaking away,
Leaving red underneath.
I open the gate. I did it. All this way by myself.
I'm home.

Nev Parkin

My House

My house is made of bricks and cement
A roof and a chimney with smoke coming through
My house has windows too
My house has a front door coloured blue
And a letterbox for the postman.
Here, we have a coal cellar beneath our kitchen floor
The coal is delivered to the back yard.
When the sirens went off during the war
The coalman left the cover off
I fell to the floor.
Then the cover was replaced -
No-one saw me there
They all went searching in the park
And I was in the cellar sucking a lump of coal.
They got the police searching -
Nowhere to be found -
Until someone came to collect the coal
From underground,
There was I
Happy, sucking this piece of coal
Sitting on the floor.
I did not know what it was -
Well I was only four.

Ron

i will know my future in april when my case is re-assessed*

It seems my bungalow is falling apart.

I hate each room.

This feeling came only when my husband died. I keep trying to teach myself to cope but feel so helpless.

I live on my own.

I lost my right arm when I lost my husband, he did everything in the house. He was a do it yourself man.

The bungalow has started to deteriorate. I don't have enough money to afford new furnishings or to pay workmen to renovate. It's a nightmare of loneliness. I have very little contact with neighbours.

I use the same mug morning and night. I never set the table.

I am on medication.

My husband even thought for me.

I'm worried about my bungalow deteriorating. I've got to the stage when I take my glasses off, to avoid seeing cracked paint.

I must have the cleanest cutlery drawer in Middlesbrough. I thoroughly cleaned one drawer, leaving all the others drawers neglected. I washed all the good quality cutlery: This was to ward off illness. It was uncharacteristic, I don't normally have the energy to do anything domestic. My husband used to share the chores, in fact he could iron better than me.

Now I haven't the heart to put things away properly. I just shove them in cupboards.

I am afraid to move, as it would cost as much to move as my bungalow is worth. My social worker suggested a Nursing Home but this reminds me of the psychiatric hospital, which made my illness worse.

Whilst staying in a psychiatric hospital, I made no progress.

I suffered emotional damage, which aggravated my condition. The absence of privacy - no separate bedroom, only curtains around the bed - and having to be among Alzheimer's patients made me worse.

Having been institutionalized made it harder to deal with the responsibility of my own home when I came out.

Audrey Nixon

There were at least fifty evacuee children in the hall at York. A lady in fine clothes pointed to me - chose me at the age of nine to live in her big house. I had my own luxurious room and was taught exactly how to hold a knife and fork. Before going there I had used only a spoon to eat my dinner.

The house was very large, and the lady, who was diabetic, had tiny scales, which looked like gold, to weigh her food on the dining table.

At Easter I was given a chocolate replica of the house.

My hosts, Mr. and Mrs. Wallace wanted to adopt me, but my father wouldn't agree. I waved them goodbye, and rejoined the big working-class family I'd been born into. I was glad to be back and did not pine, even though I was sleeping three in bed.

Audrey Nixon

Extracts From A Diary

18.9 (4 am).
A nurse came to see me about Cliff, and the possibility of his going into a nursing home - shattering thought. I couldn't keep a budgie in a cage, how can I do it to a man I've known for fifty years? They haven't all been happy or content, but what could I expect from life? I'm a coward and wish I didn't have to make the decision. Pray for help, guidance. Cannot concentrate on anything, my mind going round in circles. Cannot rest or sleep.

19.9
Went to see A and H and talked with them for an hour. Tried putting thoughts into words to get some sense. I think it helps, although tears blur the whole scene. Visited the hospital. Cliff rambles on, flashes of temper showing - more like his usual self, but talked quite reasonably to J and I. His manner changes in seconds. If only it could stay reasonable. I feel weary, cough troublesome and eyes painful.

20.9
Have an appointment to see a consultant at the hospital. Couldn't sleep worrying about it, have an awful feeling of apprehension, almost hostility. Spent half an hour trying to relax and collect my thoughts. Talked to H who assured me that I would not need to fight for Cliff.

Interview not as traumatic, as I had feared. Cliff will be there for another ten days or more, should give me a chance to pull myself together, ready for what lies ahead. Feel I should apologise to the doctor and his staff for my abruptness. It's either that or tears at present, but feel calmer now I know what is planned.

21.9
Slept a little better, coughed less. Went to town and had a good walk, though very windy. Visited hospital as usual and made to feel less than welcome - vile temper, to be expected as tranquilizers reduced. Home again, I tried reading a book, but the words just slip past my eyes. Watched TV news, which depressed me more.

22.9
Here comes autumn. Slept badly, tossing and coughing and always listening for sounds of movements. Visited hospital in the afternoon - H went with me. Cliff sitting with another patient, but hardly spoke a

word. In fact he was dozing most of the time. We were talking of places familiar to him, but very little response. It worries me when he is subdued.

23.9
Good night's sleep still eludes me. I wake after about two hours and then my mind goes racing over present and future worries. Played music and even tried to sing, but croak and cough the only sounds. So sat and relaxed a while, but memories of four years ago crowds in and spoils any benefits.

I'll try another, less poignant time. Was going out for a short walk, but rain has spoilt that idea.
I'm promising myself a day at the coast and or country this week before Cliff comes home. Perhaps tomorrow will be fine.

24.9
A bad night, one I would like to forget . Weather not too bad so I'm going out, probably to the coast.

Spent morning in Redcar. Had a fairly brisk walk about on the beach and watched the sea and gulls. Calms my mind, irons out a few nerves. Visited Cliff in evening, complaining as usual. More like his old self. Tried to reassure him that when the treatment ends and he is a little better, he will be coming home. At last managed to get my plants into the garden, just before it rained.

25.9
Up early, had appointment to see doctor. He hadn't any news of Cliff. He also suggests I think about nursing home. I feel I'm being pushed from all sides on this matter. Perhaps I should give it some thought, but I still think I must try to look after Cliff myself if at all possible, while he has some awareness at least. When I leave him after visiting, he looks so alone and forlorn. I mustn't let him down.

26.9
Another bad night, despite anti-biotic, linctus etc. A and H phoned and then came up. Sat and talked over all manner of problems. It helps to put things down or talk them out of my system - I hope. Did breathing and exercise, but succeeded in cramping my feet! Had a quick walk over to Stockton and felt fresher for it. Transport problems, so unable to visit hospital. Phone enquiry satisfactory, but I don't like to miss visiting when I had promised to be there. Gave some thought to financial and legal aspects since talk with I.W. Feel somewhat reassured to know how I stand regarding house etc.

27.9
Cough less troublesome and slept better, which helps a lot. Packed
a case with Cliff's clothes ready for discharge. Visited in afternoon
and met friends and ex-colleagues along the way, which certainly
brightened my day. Cliff his usual grumpy self. Sister will ring me
after doctor's round.

She rang in evening. Cliff coming home on Monday afternoon. Says
his face lit up when doctor told him. I don't think he believed me
when I said it wouldn't be long.

28.9
Bad night. Severe headache so got up fairly early. Went to shops for
exercise and to try and 'unwind'. Visited in afternoon and expected
Cliff to be at least pleased his discharge is arranged, but oh no – he
doesn't believe it, says the doctor is 'romancing'. He soon takes the
pleasure out of visiting. Call from Social Services, who will be
coming to see us. Reassuring to know that help will be available,
although until Cliff is home I don't know what I may need. Relaxed in
evening, tried to empty my mind of worries. Failed! S. i0nvited me to
lunch on Sunday – such good friends.

29.9
Slept better. Did some washing and then took things easy. Relaxed
in warm bath and then dozed off, woke up, water cold – silly thing to
do. Visited Cliff and took his clothes to convince him he'll be coming
home soon.
Still doesn't believe me. He's rather quiet, talking in a whisper, and
very little to say.

Sunday 30.9
Today I planned to do things to satisfy myself, so spent the morning
sewing and thinking of odd things, not really concentrating. The
morning was gone before I realized – no lunch prepared, but not
bothered. Rain stopped, so planted a few bulbs, different kinds –
something to look forward to in the Spring. Watched some TV,
possibly last chance for a while, unless Cliff has changed.

Monday 1.10
This is the day Cliff comes home from hospital. I've been awake half
the night worrying about how he'll be. I don't know what I expected
but he is just as grumpy as usual, perhaps even more confused and
stubborn. Took an hour to get him to bed – he insists the kitchen is
the toilet and bathroom. After a night's sleep he may be better.
Managed stairs quite well.

2.10

My 'holiday' is over, and with a vengeance – a large stack of bedding to wash! Cliff very difficult to get up and dressed. Cliff visited by friends and Dr. Murdoch's nurse, and spoke fairly sensibly, but by teatime became more confused and aggressive. Very hard to talk to and try to calm him. I took 'refuge' by chopping a bush almost to the ground. I felt a bit better. Relaxed for about an hour before going to bed.

31.10

Up early, but Cliff not so difficult. Still, it took one and a half hours to get him washed and ready for his Day Centre. A visit from Home Help Services, then a quick dash to town and a brisk walk made me feel fresher. Cliff reasonable when he came home, but after tea started rambling, then difficult to get to bed. By that time the benefit of my walk and rest after lunch were more or less lost. I'll try again tomorrow.

4.10

An awful day, I can't write tonight.

5.10

A quieter start to the day. Cliff ready and off to Day Centre. I had a quick dash to the bank, etc, worked off some of my frustrations.

All the benefits of relaxing and concentrating on calming influences are wiped out by yesterday's events, or so it seems at present. I'll just have to try again.
Sat watching the wind toss the tops of the trees, almost like semaphore. Lovely cloud effect.

Blanche Wallace

The Dolls' House

On the table with a bow tied round it - a dolls' house just for me. Green metal windows with leaded lights, and a door with a number and a handle. The walls outside looked just like red brick, with a roof and a chimney all made out of wood.

I opened the front - my eyes lit up - inside there were rooms of different sizes.

On the top floor there's a little bedroom with a doll lying down, and teddy bears and toys, and in the corner, a baby and some little clothes. In the next room there's a big double bed, even a wardrobe and sets of drawers, and bedside cabinets with lamps upon them, and even a book to read.

There's another bedroom done in pink, all pretty and cosy for a little girl, with a pram to push and toys to play with, and shelves full of dolls, books and games. And there's a bathroom with a sink and bath, silver taps that turn round and round, with a toilet in the corner and you could lift the seat up. Even little towels hanging off hooks.

Down the stairs there's a sitting room with a three-piece suite in front of a fire that was painted on the wall. There's little ornaments all around, and on the mat a dog in a basket, and a television set all made of wood with knobs to turn.

There's a dining room with a table and chairs, and place-mats with knives and forks at each side; plastic plates, cups and saucers, pretend food in serving dishes, and all around the wall, cabinets with hidden treasures inside.

In the kitchen there are cupboards and worktops with a bread bin, a toaster and little wooden spoons, a cooker with a door that opened out, and pots and pans you could pretend to cook. There's a washer in the corner, with an iron and ironing board hidden in a cupboard in the wall.

In the house there were some figures you could move from room to room. You could take the furniture out, and change it around. All the rooms had carpets and curtains, even wallpaper on the walls.

Close the door now and go to bed, and tomorrow start again - changing the furniture, moving the figures, bathing the baby and changing its clothes. I can dust and hoover my little doll's house, because it's full of secrets and they're all my very own.

Kathryn

When my wife was in her late sixties, she developed Alzheimer's. She used to belong to a social club, and one day she came back early, she said the other women had sent her home, saying something was wrong.

The doctor put her on tablets, but it didn't do any good, so she went for psychiatric assessment. At one point the psychiatrist went out of the room and she turned to me and said, "Let's go home, this feller's crackers!"

She went into hospital for a three-week assessment; I went to see her twice every day, and she always wanted to come back home. Once she turned a bit funny and accused me of seeing another woman – I said, "I'm not shot of you yet, I don't want another one."

They said she should go into a home, but I was adamant against it. You see, she had been born in a 'Home' - really it was the workhouse, we used to call it 'The Grubber'. She had been a good woman all her life, and I couldn't see her end up her days as she had begun them. I sometimes think it was the harshness of her early life that led to the illness.

I argued with the doctors and social workers; when I was young I would have fought a lion, but this time I got my son in to help, he's got a bit of the blether. He told them that I would take her home, where she belonged and where she wanted to be.

I had her at home for quite a few years after that. Sometimes it was like being at sea – we saw the sun come up, and we saw the sun go down. We had a lot on – our son had a stroke, and for a time he would come to us for the day, and my brother and I used to walk him about, to try to get him mobile. My brother's gone now.

My wife used to like to watch videos of Irish dancing, I used to buy her big boxes of dolly mixtures or Cadbury's Roses, and sometimes a big bottle of scotch, and she kept pretty happy. A neighbour used to come and sit with her so I could go to church on a Sunday, I planted her garden with flowers as a Thankyou, it could have won prizes. My wife's sisters used to visit, and one of her nieces did her hair every week, she was always proud of her hair.

I took over all the running of the household. When I was young my mother used to like to stand out in the front street gossiping, so sometimes I finished cooking the dinner, and I picked up bits and pieces that way.

We got most of our groceries delivered and kept it in the outhouse, but once we had a thief who helped himself to all our stock.

Sometimes she could be difficult; now and then she would 'disappear' and say, "Who are you, bathing me?" but then she'd relax and say, "Oh, it's our Chrissie." You have to know how to handle people, you have to go round their corner. Then she started to disappear for real, we couldn't get clothes to fit her.

When it got to the last three weeks I knew she was dying, I could see it in her eyes. On the last day of her life her sister and daughter-in-law gave her a bath, and made her comfy, and then she told them her complete life story. She was completely lucid, and afterwards they said Catherine Cookson couldn't have written it.

After she died, I woke up one night and she was standing in the corner of the bedroom, shrouded in light. She was dressed in a blue suit, and she had a ruffle round her neck, like a choirboy. Her hair was immaculate, and her figure was perfect, back to what it had been. I don't know how long she had been standing there, but then it seemed like she pressed a button and just went out the door. All the thoughts and worries I had had about her disappeared after that. It made life different for me, I knew she was safe and sound, and maybe with the way the world is, she's better off where she is.

People say to me, 'you did your duty by her', but I did it out of love, not duty. We were married over fifty years. We got married during the war, and we were bombed on our wedding day and she asked me if I wanted to run away, but I said, "No, I'm stopping here with you."

Mr.C.McLoughlin

but at night,
I can be scared to turn
on a light.

I'll say a bit about life when I was young, practically 100 years ago. Mother was the head of the household, father went to work at 6 or 6.30, and did not come home till evening. Kids had breakfast and then off to school, and those under four stayed in the house or out to play. Mother had to shop for all, and arranged food for all the family.

Monday was special, it was washday – the hardest day of the week. It all had to be done by hand; scrubbing, rinsing and hanging out, if the weather was suitable. If not, everything was hung around the fire. Ironing came next; the irons were heated round the fire. Mending and darning followed.

The weeks and the seasons went by – that, in a nutshell, was my early years.

Now, at 102, I can look back and see the difference – the vast difference. Now, everything is laid on – if you have the money. Meals are no bother, even if you're on your own. A cup of tea is my breakfast, plus a cigarette. The morning newspaper is delivered, followed soon after by the post. I keep up with the news, and decipher the code-word puzzle - that takes anything from half an hour to two hours, depending how difficult it is. That keeps my brain from stagnation. Then the usual offices – toilet, a wash and shave, make my bed, and wash up.

One or two mornings a week the cleaner comes and makes the house respectable, and every Thursday the nurse sees that I have a bath and change underwear.

If I wish to go out, and I do, my escort comes in her car and we go out for a meal with a drink. If I'm not going out, then the frozen foods come every Thursday, and there is a hot meal with a sweet; put it in the oven for 35 minutes and Hey Presto! Already there, is a can of beer and a glass of red wine.

I am also supplied with books delivered from the library – not much fiction, I prefer scientific works. Two or three times a week I play bridge with three ladies and we have two gents who look on – they are wanting to learn to play.

If I wanted to I could have my laundry done by the Social Service. It is all so easy now, you can be independent and enjoy life, which I do.

Sometimes my friends and relatives from a distance away come for a day, and we gossip and exchange news of the present and old days. Once a year I return their visit, a trip of 200 miles, I am taken there and brought back. Every time I say goodbye to them, I say this will be the last time that I will be able to travel, but when the time comes again, I am fit and ready to go and have a good time.

That reminds me, my right eye had an implant 15 years ago, and every time I see the specialist he says he'll see me again in a year's time, and so far I have! Things are not so good with my ears, though. When I play bridge, I have to watch the lips of the other players for a clue, but I manage. Sometimes, when the phone (and that's another blessing!) rings, if the caller knows my difficulty they may just shout into the receiver, to my distress. But I have found a way to converse with and listen to any visitor – I find that if my visitor sits beside me on my left and speaks naturally, I have no bother. I have a friend who is a doctor, and I have not had need of him professionally for a year and long beyond.

Once a week I go shopping with my escort, and once a fortnight I call at the bank to replenish my wallet, for my twenty cigarettes a day. I have made an arrangement with the bank for my escort to collect my cash in case I am unable to go, but up to now I haven't used her, except to listen to the clerk. All my bills are paid by Direct Debit, so I don't have to worry about remembering payments.

The only thing that upsets me about being 102 is that I have lost so many old friends and relatives. Every evening I search the death notices in the Hartlepool Mail to see if another has gone; but you can't have it all ways, and the Mail does publish my letters punctiliously. Another sad thing is when my escort takes me to visit old friends in old peoples' homes – it really distresses me. I see people decline even further as soon as they go in. Before you know where you are, they've lost interest, they're gaga, and they're on their way out.

So there you have it, perhaps not in a nutshell, but that's how I celebrate my independence.

Mr.Dickinson

When young and living in a small village in Devon, and having lost our Dad, we moved from a small-holding in the country, to a two-bedroomed terrace house. The village was on a main road and we would encounter many homeless people, mainly men, war veterans, who would knock on everyone's door to beg for food, or for money to take them on their way.

Many times the village children would find little places down the lanes, where the men had slept, and where they left their scraps and the ashes from a fire they had lit to warm themselves.

I recollect them calling and asking for help, and my mother saying," Now this is good food so enjoy it", and as she turned away, she would comment to us children, "We have to be grateful, we all have a soul".

Our home was small, but my mother made it very homely and comfortable, always a nice warm fire in the stove, and cosy in bed with hot water bottles. In those days widows and children's pensions were very little after losing the bread-winner. The priorities were to pay for the roof over your head, to pay for your food, and for the coal to keep a good fire for your warmth. If you could afford nothing else, you wore any pass-downs in the family.

There were not many hostels for homeless people then, as there are today, only something called the work-house. Beggars, known as "tramps", got no hand out from the Government as people as do today.

I can see my mother talking of her past life (during the First World War), when her husband was killed fighting in France, and she was left with a baby son. She was then living at home with her mother and her father. Unfortunately, her mother died and soon after her father married again which did not work out for her. She had to leave home and find a job to support her and her son, which she found heartbreaking, and it made her homeless.

She had to look for employment, and with her son in mind she found a position with a man, a widower with two daughters. She became their housekeeper, caring for the girls, cleaning, cooking and baking, everything a mother would do for her own family.

After many months of this they decided to marry and went to Scotland. My father had been a naval officer, and coming out of the First World War, he took a post in the Coast Guard Station on the outskirts of Aberdeen. Two more daughters and his son were born.

For reasons unknown to me, they came down to the outskirts of a little village in Devon, to a smallholding, where three of us children walked a mile and a half to the village school. We took our lunch satchels with us, and every Sunday we walked a mile and a half to the village church, to Sunday School.

The two stepsisters took jobs in service, living in, as they did in those days. My father used to kill rabbits and pigeons for the local farmers. During one of these outings, he got up on the hedge to shoot pigeons, carrying the gun on his shoulder, when it accidentally went off, shooting the side of his face off, and killing him outright.

I remember returning from school with my sister and older brother, walking in to the kitchen where my mother was baking for Christmas. My youngest brother, just four years old, had been with my father. He was curled up my in my dad's wooden high-backed chair with arm rests, with his eyes tightly closed. My mother explained what had happened, asking us to stay with him while she would go to the cottages at the bottom of the lane to get some help.

After many hours – midnight - my father's body was found and laid in a cart in a shed. I remember the coffin laying our sitting room until his funeral when it was covered with a Union Jack from the British Legion, and taken on a horse and cart the mile and a half to the church.

Being just six years old, I did not attend my dad's funeral, I recall sitting by the fire in the big black stove, feeling very sad in my young mind, and not knowing what to expect. We were asked to my mother's brother's home in London for Christmas, a very long train journey in those days. It was around Christmas Eve, and that evening they were new pyjamas and slippers warming by a lovely fire, and lovely presents on Xmas morning. Lovely meals in the dining room, so nicely laid out with nice serviettes for those days!

One day we went to Finsbury Park rolling in the snow with our cousin, and another day we went to Madame Tussaud's so wonderful and bewildering.

On our return home I took ill with yellow jaundice and had my bed brought downstairs while I was ill - eight weeks. I remember the doctor calling so far out into the country, and sitting on my bed letting me hear his wrist watch ticking!

I felt so weak and looked so yellow. It is still very vivid - missing my dad so much and wanting my mother near me, so frightened to be without her. For many years I would cry myself to sleep, praying she would not die too.

Eventually we left the small holding and rented a two-bedroomed terraced house in the village, so happy to be nearer school and the local church, not missing my previous home at all.

We had a very big cupboard underneath the staircase, so my mother set up a little house shop, having shelves fitted for all the jars and boxes of sweets and groceries. I recall the agent for Lyons and Hornimans tea calling with a lovely big van, and the makes of sweets, many still sold today. Also cigarettes and tobacco, knitting wool, needles, sewing needles and pins, knitting patterns, reels of cottons, ladies stockings, so very many things!

Our living room was closed off by curtains drawn right across for privacy at meal times, and bath night on a Friday with a clothes horse around the bath, draped with a blanket to keep us private.

Once a month mother would go to Barnstable to pay the wholesalers' bills, on a weekly bus that came through the village. She would also make her own ice-cream, so enjoyed by the villagers. She sometimes served it in the house, in small glass dishes, and with cornets and wafers. We were very close to the village green where the school children would build up a huge bonfire for November 5th, and my mam sold all kinds of fireworks and sparklers. They could not be obtained in the other two shops in the village. I was frightened of the 'jumping jacks!'

My mother did not make a great profit in those days - things were so cheap, and as vans came from the nearby town, people would say "I can get this or that for a half-penny cheaper from them". She would stay open until late at night for customers.

I loved being in the church choir, every Sunday morning and evening, and Sunday Schools in the afternoons. My village school had just fifty pupils and my headmistress was so knowledgeable. She taught every subject including music, maths (fractions, decimals and much more), history, geography, and dictation (which I loved), essays, religion, and so many various things, including singing with the tuning fork!

I remember a yearly concert in the village hall, a lovely church supper once a year with fancy dress, a dance at the hall. Oh, I did love my village life, and I had such a kind and caring mother, wonderful when any of us children were poorly. The vicar would call at our house shop and always ask my mother is she would "sell me to him", I was so frightened that she would!

The choir would go to the Vicarage and sing carols at Christmas, and go and play croquet with him on his lawn at the appropriate time of the year. Again I was "his Little blue" as I had the blue mallet. He meant it all in the nicest possible way, but being about eight or nine years old, I was naturally slightly nervous, when I suppose I should have felt rather proud!

Sadly he was to pass away, and a new vicar came to the village, a very nice gentleman also, who would occasionally come to my mother's shop.

I think I was about twelve years old when my eldest brother left school, and as my stepsister was working for a family of millers in Cornwall, he became the bread-winner. We left the village in Devon and went to Cornwall.

At twenty-two I was sent on war work to Gloucester, eventually returning home and moving with my mother to Middlesbrough, where I met and married my husband.

I still love Devon and the people.

Pat Lowes

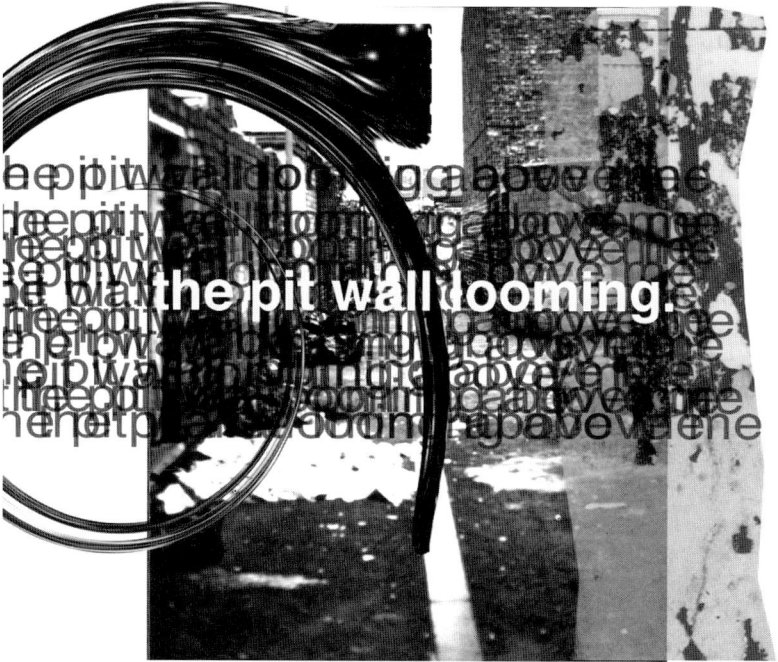

the pit wall looming.

Cupboards

I stared into my open cupboard, it was full of different plastic bottles and pressurised spray cans of polish, bathroom cleaner, kitchen cleaner, window cleaner, oven cleaner, even little packets of disinfectant wipes and anti-bacterial washing up liquid. What would my grandma say? Not to mention my great grandma.

My mind went back to the early 50's when I was a little girl. I would go with my mum to visit my great Grandma and mum would do her cleaning. Grandma's house had a very large oak front door with brass door furnishings that mum polished for her each week. Inside, the hall was very dark, we would walk past the parlour on the right, the door was always shut, and it was like a secret room where children were never allowed.

We would then go into the kitchen. As you went into the room, the first thing that met your eyes was an extremely large, dark wood dresser full of beautiful blue and white china which I was never allowed to touch. Opposite us was another door that lead into the scullery, across the door was a red velvet curtain that kept out the draft on a night; next to the door was a small window, also draped with a red velvet curtain, which looked out onto a neatly kept back yard.

In the yard there was a coal shed, a toilet with a wooden seat and little pieces of newspaper threaded together with a length of string, and hooked over a rusty nail. In the corner of the yard was a large wooden barrel under a drainpipe, this was used to catch the rainwater that grandma would use to wash her hair. In another corner of the yard was a wooden tub used for the washing, inside the tub was a poss stick, and above it was a wringer also made of wood.

The door from the yard led into the tiny scullery, it had a large grey stone sink that stood on two small brick walls; in it sat a metal bucket and a piece of carbolic soap. There was only one cold-water tap, high up on the wall. The sink was only about four inches deep, so it could only be used to rest your bowl or bucket in. A small kitchen table always stood next to it, covered in flour. There was a wonderful smell of freshly baked bread coming from her small black oven. It was Friday and that meant baking day. Next to the table was a pantry, full of home-made jam and chutney, large stone jars of flour and I'd never seen so much pepper - Grandma said it was in case of another war. She also squashed a large metal boiler into her tiny scullery, used to boil her whites.

In the kitchen there was a large black lead fireplace, with another oven. On the hearth there would be big brown bowls filled with dough and a lovely warm coal fire in the grate. Standing on its end at the edge of the hearth, was an old cast-iron iron that grandma would have to heat on the fire to do her ironing. Next to the iron stood a brass companion set, of a very long handled brush, shovel, rake and poker. A brass fender surrounded the hearth. The fire heated a tank of water at the side of it, and this was fitted with a little tap. On the top of the fireplace was a brass rod holding up a red velvet pelmet.

On the mantle shelf there were two very big green pot vases; in the centre stood Grandad's retirement clock, made of oak, and a plaque with his name on. Just to one side of the clock was an urn containing the ashes of their son, Bill. At the other side of the clock was Grandad's pipe rack. At one side of the fire Grandad would sit in his big carved oak rocking chair, he sat on a beautiful tapestry cushion, depicting a typical English country garden with a tall, elegant lady in a crinoline dress. Behind his back was a cream cotton cushion, hand-embroidered with pretty little blue and pink flowers. Next to his chair was a set of three deep drawers with a cupboard above; in the bottom drawer he kept all his tools and materials, for cobbling the family's shoes.

Behind his chair, attached to the wall, was a wooden box with a mirror above, this is where they kept their brushes and combs. Sometimes Grandma would bring in a dining chair from the parlour; she would sit down and take out the big bone hair-pin from her hair. I would run, full of great excitement, to the box on the wall to find her hairbrush. When she let down her hair it reached the floor. I was so small I could never reach the top of her head. I thought she was like Rapunzel. Her hair was still very dark although she was in her later years. It had a wonderful shine. She said it was because she washed it in rain-water and liquid paraffin.

When I'd finished, she would take it to one side, plait it, wind it up round and round on top of her head, then without looking in the mirror, put back the large bone pin, and it always looked perfect. This influenced me in later life to brush my daughter's hair correctly, and to teach her the same thing as instructed by my grandma.

Usually Grandma would sit at the other side of the fire; at night she kept herself busy with her needlework or knitting. Her chair was smaller, pale green with an antimacassar on the back and matching arm covers, all made from old sheets and embroidered with the same pretty little flowers as Grandad's cushion. Above Grandma's chair was a small shelf, on it sat a large brown wireless; this had a battery inside that Grandad had to take to a shop every week, to be charged up. Under the window was a table covered with a dark red velvet tablecloth and two benches either side. I think Grandma liked red velvet!

Grandma would sit me at the table, and teach me how to manicure my nails. When it was time for a meal it was off with the velvet cloth, and on with a white linen one, then as soon as the table was cleared, it was back on with the velvet. Also in the room was a red velvet chaise longue; I would lay across it, pretending I was a princess, although it made me wriggle about because the horsehair it was filled with, would prickle my legs and bottom. Grandma would ask my mum if I had worms!

On the floor were two multicoloured hooky mats, made by my great grandparents from old bits of material; coats were the best as they were harder wearing.

I wonder what they all would say, if they could see in my cupboard today.

Christine Nicholson

My House

My house is a three bedroomed semi-detached
With a black iron garden gate
Which leads to a long garden
Filled with rosebushes,
And at the moment winter pansies are flowering.
My house has a white front door
With white windowsills
Which I manage to keep very clean
As they are PVC.

Here is the room where I spend most of my time,
Here I can settle down and really relax,
Feel that I am at peace with myself.
Here I get constant sunshine
And feel a great sense of joy.

A wonderful photograph
Of my three grandchildren together
Is smashing to look at.
It is on the side plinth of the fireplace,
A space holding photographs of family
Son, daughter-in-law,
Daughter, son-in-law
And the photo of my dog
I had for thirteen years,
Who I loved very much.

Gwen

I never knew my birth mother or my father. I was put into care when I was two weeks old, I was in a nursery, and then I to Welburn Hall Boarding School, Kirbymoorside. In the holidays I went to a foster family, I liked it there, and I used to get upset when it was time to return to school.

When I was 15 I was living with the family, but my foster Dad got poorly and things started to go wrong, I went a bit haywire, I suppose. I was taken to a psychiatrist who put me on Largactil – I wasn't really mentally ill, but I had bad nerves from my childhood. I had suffered at school, one of the staff had interfered with me, but I didn't understand and I never spoke up, not like now when everyone talks about it. I didn't know anything, I didn't know what periods were until I started.

I went into St.Luke's Hospital at 15, and I saw things no young person should see, it was quite horrific. I stayed there for 12 years, I did a life sentence.

After that I was moved from one place to another. I was on the Largactil which made me into a different person from what I am now – the medication was so strong that I could sleep the clock round, and when I did wake up I was violent and nasty.

At 30 I went to Blenheim House to live. I was like a little girl, I hadn't grown up, and I was very attention seeking.

When I was 36 they realised that my eyes were being affected by the medication, and stopped it. They took me off it over five weeks; this was after being on it for twenty years. I couldn't understand why I felt so bad, I had a hell of a year, I wanted to end it all. The staff seemed to shout at me morning, noon and night, which made me worse.

Once, the matron called the doctor in, and he threatened me with another mental hospital; that played on my mind, and things went from bad to worse. I ended up in North Tees Hospital, I had a lovely doctor there, but he put me on another drug, and I was just as bad as before.

Then I was at Sunningdale, and through a lot of hard work I managed to get myself off almost all the medication, although I still wasn't mentally healthy. I had behavioural problems, through not growing up in a normal way.

A brilliant social worker helped me to get a flat, and to start living independently – I was petrified, I thought I couldn't make it on my own. Now I've been there 13 years, the longest I've been anywhere. It's wonderful, I live on my own and I've got lots of friends now.

I'm on a minimum of medication now, but I'll have to stay on that for the rest of my life. I still don't know what it is to have a normal night's sleep, and I've got a lot of anger about what's been taken away from me.

I attend the Lansdowne Day Centre, and they've helped me a lot, I get involved in lots of meetings and different things. I like to do my own thing at home, I watch TV, clean up, do crochet. I feel super in my flat, I really feel I've accomplished something. I give talks about my life to other people, to try and encourage them to live independently like me. It's been very hard, but I've done it.

I think it's a different world now, I think it's lovely - well, it is for me. I've got my flat, my friends, and my own life. Every year I'm changing, I'm growing, and I don't need so much help. I'm doing an NVQ, and giving talks to people. I don't want to keep harping on – 'poor me' – this story has a happy ending, so positive.

June Taylor

acidic smells of burning plastic and copper wire.
...oing home for tea.

Grandad's Army Soup

Home
is the warm comforting smell
of Grandad's army soup
He would use an old mincer
and mince all that he could find
>Like
>Onions
>Carrots
>Potatoes
>Bacon
>Pork chops
And different meats chopped up
and thrown in.
He would say
WASTE NOTHING
that's what I was taught
in the army when I was a chef.
But of course
he was also a Scot.

Ian

Living Alone

I'm 50. I live in a high-rise block of flats, it has its advantages, but it also has a lot of disadvantages, depending on how many friends or what outside resources and support you've got. It can be quite isolated.

Living in a block is not like when I was a child in the olden days, or so called olden days - there was community spirit. Of course, then I lived in a house with my parents, sisters and younger brother. And of course, in those days the neighbors used to sit on the front steps in the warm weather, chatting away in the gardens, while the children were playing, probably eating jam and bread. There may be some of those days left, but certainly not in a block of flats.

In these flats there are 16 storeys, I was on the 3rd floor when I first came, in number 34, now I'm in number 4. When I was in 34, I just covered it up because I went out drinking. I always used to remember that song: -

Four walls to hear me,
Four walls to see,
Four walls surrounding me,
Closing in on me –

it was sung by Jim Reeves. So I used the excuse, who wants to sit in the four walls, so I would go to the club and drink and look for company. But of course, by 1987 that changed because of my drink problem, I decided I didn't want to drink anymore and got sober. So obviously, they were fair-weather friends; I lost quite a bit of sociability, or did I, because sometimes I was drinking alone towards the end.

I have a good supportive family, so I'm lucky in that respect, especially one of my sisters and my nieces, who help me in many ways, such as for cleaning up, and bit of shopping. But when you are alone, when you open that door, especially since I've come into number 4 in October 1991, I've become more isolated.

Some evenings when you're feeling okay, and you've got the cultivated right attitude towards your own company, and you feel good in yourself, you're okay, you can get on with things, you can read a book, listen to a tape, listen to a CD, listen to a play on the radio, and escape into that, and enjoy it. A lot of the time I like escaping into books because it takes me away from how I am and how I'm feeling, but still I'm left with me.

Once that big door closes, and I turn that lock closed, I'm locked in. Sometimes I feel like it is a prison, and when I go out to do the shopping, or go to the Day Centre, or for a meal with one of my family, I feel I'm on parole. But once I turn the key, open that door, slam that door shut, and bolt it, then I'm back in, like a prisoner in my cell.

It isn't that bad though, because I have a phone. I think without a phone and a communicative voice I would be totally lost, I would be totally isolated, cut off, I think I would just not want to be here. But to pick up the phone, with understanding people who are very close, and you can talk to them about how you feel, or they can talk to you, you can get a perspective of reality and just what reality is. That being, that many people these days live alone, are isolated, even in houses. There were times when I was isolated, even in a crowd, and still can be. Isolation comes through your own feelings and the way you feel about yourself, and about everything else - you can isolate yourself.

We have a little bit of communication, perhaps in the laundry, but it's only passers-by, ships in the night, as I would call them. You can get the odd one talking to you as you are doing your clothes. Sometimes you can stand with the odd Concierge, who will let you talk to them in the passage.

So in a sense it can be a prison, or it can be a joy, a home, depending how you look at it. Some days for me it's a home, some days after coming from the Centre or from group therapy, or even just from shopping, I want to be alone, I want to be with the books. But of late, I think I'm closing myself off, and just pushing myself into this flat, and isolating myself completely.

I'm not using the phone as much as I used to, it's as though I'm afraid to face that outside world. A part of me feels safe cocooned in my flat, no one to bother me, no worries, but I don't believe that is healthy. I believe in facing up to your feelings and your fears, and also your confidences, and taking support and help from other people. Inter-relating is a good thing, but it's hard, it depends on how you have done it, I think when you are alone sometimes it's very, very difficult.

I've had a couple of relationships, I had one who stayed with me for a while, who had never stayed with me before, and suddenly wanted to stay with me for a few days. I felt as though my privacy was invaded after the first day or so, I was vulnerable inside. I don't think I could have lived with that person, although I loved that person; I don't think I could have that person with me day in day out, once the novelty wore off, it just seemed that it wasn't for me. And yet on the other hand I suppose I would like someone to share my flat and share the positive things with me, like good Christian books I read, listen to music etc.

I would like someone to be with me, someone who I could support and they could support me, it would feel a bit better, but of course that's dreaming, who knows if that's my future, but we can all dream.

Everybody seems to be suspicious of each other, when they talk nice to you in the passage, they seem wonderful, but there is a lot of gossip that goes round. The block of flats down the road from me has a community place, a lounge where you can have coffee; most of the residents are elderly. I am thinking of moving when I get myself a bit more sorted out, moving to the block down the road, because there is the odd flat available still, but yet on the other hand I will still be taking *me,* and it will be all about how I feel.

As I come to the end of this script, I am grateful that I have communication through the phone. My brother lives in this block of flats on the 1st floor - now he is deaf and dumb, so in a sense he is in a more isolated world than me. He can see, he can ride a bike and he's got his full vision no problem, but he has no speech or full communication like I have. So when you think of it, he's only mixing with his own kind, and he is segregated off. For him to be understood, you need to be really close to him, or to know a bit of the signs. When I'm talking to him I think I only get half the stuff. So what really fills me with gratitude when I start feeling down and feeling alone, and when I'm spending many hours my myself, I think I have a lot of blessings to count, at least I can communicate and hear. So therefore, although I haven't got full vision, I suppose there are people more isolated then myself.

It is good little flat where I am, it's comfortable little place, I've got nice furniture and a nice table etc, I would say my home is pretty reasonable, pretty clean. It's an open door, anybody would be welcome, anybody who became my friend would be welcome, though I can be a little bit suspicious. The good thing is, we are on an intercom system here now, it's a lot better than when I first came, and there was no security. When someone comes to visit me I often joke that it's like Alcatraz.

But it's attitude really, living alone is quite difficult, sometimes it feels like solitary confinement, despite day centres and phones. But it's how you are feeling inside of yourself, because you can be at home wherever you are. I never thought I could live alone, because before I left my parents I was totally dependent on them. When they died and I had to live by myself, well, it was a different thing. If it hadn't been for someone helping me in 1985, I wouldn't have been able to open a tin, or butter a piece of bread, that's how bad I was. If it hadn't been for this lady taking me in and helping me, I dare say I would be hopeless now, I would have to have a carer in, or maybe be in a home.

I have a lot of things to be thankful for, a lot of gratitude, but of late I am feeling quite isolated. Some days you can feel really lonely, and don't live in reality, because you live in your head. Then you have to look at your needs, and not your wants, and you feel a lot better, and you can feel comfortable in your home, this is how it is for me in this flat.

I have started to go back to cleaning up again and taking more responsibility in the cleaning, this is because I caused a bit of a problem for my niece. I feel proud of myself when I get it done, I'm looking after this place, I'm taking responsibility. It isn't easy, you can become lazy when you are by yourself. I go from the television to the radio to the music to a book, and I'm just going round and round in that circle.

This is my little castle and I'm happy in it, and try to get on with it. They say someone else's patch looks better; the grass is always greener on the other side. Life is certainly what we make it. I've still got friends, and the Day Centre, otherwise I would be totally on my own.

I have no debts, it's a rental flat. The rent, the electricity, and the phone bill are all paid. I have my food, I'm secure, what more do I need, except the happiness and contentment.

Ray Bage

I am a twenty-five year old woman with cerebral palsy, I like to enjoy myself like anyone else – I like clubbing, drinking, socialising, all kinds of sports and keep-fit, I'll try anything. I don't let my disability get in the way of what I want to do.

But I know that if I wasn't disabled I would have left home before now. My Dad died a few years ago – he was disabled too – but I never asked him what he thought about it all, he died when I was too young. I think my Mum is over-protective of me – I've tried to talk to her about moving out and setting up on my own, but she thinks I'll find it hard, and she tries to put me off. I say I know it will be hard, but it's important to be independent and to grow up and take that step.

Everyone has to learn to cook and all that, but it's taken me longer because my Mum has done everything for me. Once, when I was younger, I made myself beans on toast – I made it OK, but then, when I was carrying it through, my hand slipped and the beans went all over the wall! Still, it's all part of learning, and now I do more for myself than my brother does, and he's able-bodied.

When my Dad died, it made me realise that my family couldn't always be there for me, so I have to learn to do as much for myself as I can.

I'd like a bungalow, with lilac-coloured walls, and nice fashionable curtains and stuff, and I'd invite my Mum round, and then I'd cook for her.

I've done wall-climbing and abseiling, I've got a tattoo and my belly-button pierced, and I'm planning to go sky-diving, and I've done the great North Run five times, so I really think I can learn to run a home.

Jill Conway

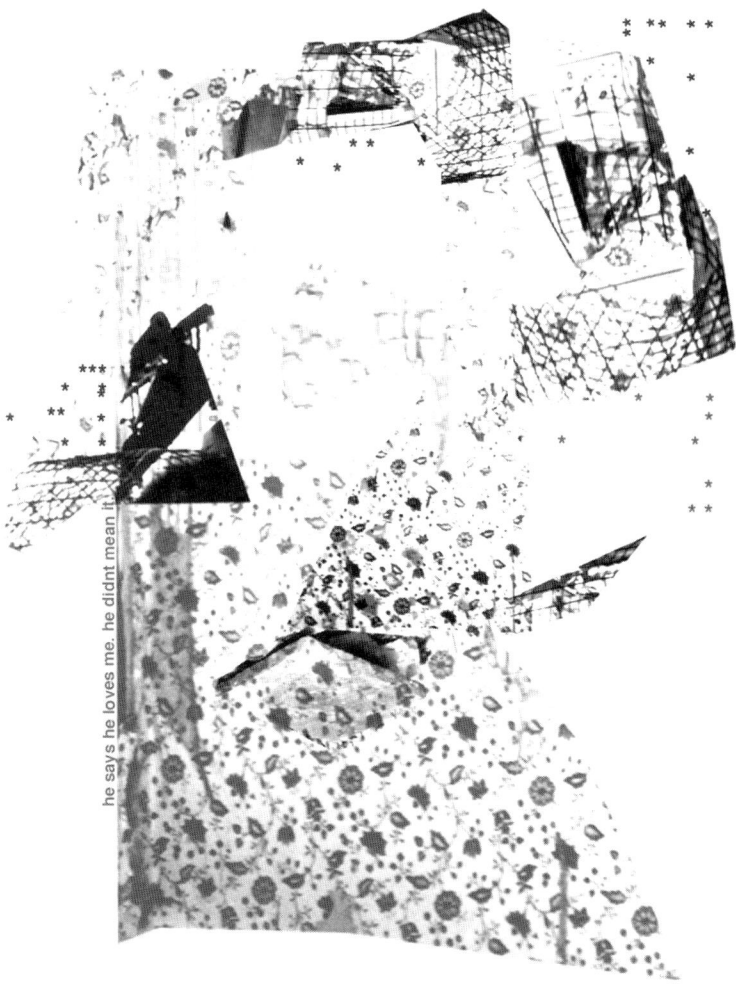

he says he loves me. he didnt mean it

I lived with my family until I was 16, and then in Blenheim House, a residential home for people with physical disabilities.

But I wanted to be more independent. I needed more scope to be who I really am, and to live my life the way that I want to live it. I felt that the home was putting a damper on my personality.

So now I'm in the Endeavour Independent Living Project and I can make myself a hot drink, using a kettle tipper and a liquid level indicator.

I want to live like other people. I want to be able, not disabled!

I like it better on my own. In the home, there was no privacy, and I felt like I lived in a box! Strangers could walk in and out. They can't do that here because I keep the door locked, but I feel less safe, especially at night. But I have my privacy and independence now, and to me that's a price worth paying and I'll never give it up. It's a good job I'm brave!

I would like to live in a normal street with gardens, that doesn't have 'disabled' written all over it. With noisy neighbours and kids playing outside.

The housing people have been to do some repairs this week, but they've only done half a job. They haven't fixed the dripping tap – I can't hear it, but I can see it dripping, and I can see it on my water bill!

I can stay here for two years, then I want to move on to more independent living, with less support. My Mum and Dad think this is perfect for me, but I want to move on, I think they are a bit over-protective. But at the end of the day I know they will always be there for me, I want to do them proud!

I've been living here for six months now and I'm much happier. Although I get bored, it won't be for much longer, because I'm organising extra care staff, so that I can go out.

My biggest goal so far is to get off benefits, and it seems the most impossible.

I have been put in touch with the Shaw Trust. They can assess you and find out what you can do, not just what you can't, and then help you to build up existing skills, or train you to work.

Some people say my life is perfect, because I don't have to work. But I really want to earn my own keep. That's what I call independence!

Terri Phoenix

"CASA", it means "Home or House" in Italian, and I was born in Venice - Italy.

I sometimes don't feel quite sure where "home" is. Is it my birthplace or the place of my adoption? Naturally, a transition had to be made all those years ago - 55 of them to be precise, where from the "palace" I used to live, I moved to a dingy back room in Hartlepool. (I'll add that a 'palace' in Venice is a large, tall building, and we were fortunate enough to have a big apartment on the top floor. My father was a master upholsterer and decorator; he worked on the maintenance of churches, embassies and hotels. Also, his pride and joy was the upkeep of the interior decorations of the famous Venice Opera House, which was to be destroyed by fire in 1996.)

What a difference in life-style! But this I did in the name of "love". I had been an interpreter during the occupation of Venice by the British Forces back in 1946, and that is how I met my boss, now my husband, Sam.

I remember one evening, only about two months after my arrival, going to the pictures and feeling very sad, as the newsreel was still showing pictures concerning the war. At the end they played the National Anthem, then everybody, as one , stood up to the victorious sound. Then I cried, yes I did cry, here the people had the right to be proud of their country. I didn't have a royal family, they went into exile, the country was governed by communists, what did I have? It was then that I felt I belonged here. I too stood up to the music. I too was part of this country, this was "home" for me now. But then I was young and still yearning for my mam and dad, and the streets of Venice were beckoning me back again. I sank into a kind of sadness.

The only place where I retained a sense of belonging was when I went to Church. There, everybody, as in the cinema, became one body only, one voice, but this time for the love of God, and praying aloud in Latin, I calmed down. I was at "home", with its familiar ways and sounds.

Time passed. I had two sons, and I had to assert the fact that, although my accent was very strong, I did have a brain. I found a job, then a better one, and then I was offered the position of Lecturer in Italian at the local technical college, and at two more colleges. For two hours, twice a week I was at "home" again, but this time it was my "Casa", the place of my youth.

Did I betray my adopted place? Did I neglect my sense of gratitude? I don't know. But that was then.

I am old now, well retired, and I know where "HOME" is. It is here, in this land where I choose to live and die, the land that I love so much because it is true what they say, that "HOME" is where the heart is.

Maria Wright